Jo Shapcott was born in London. Poems from her three award-winning collections *Electroplating the Baby* (1988), *Phrase Book* (1992) and *My Life Asleep* (1998) are gathered in a selected poems, *Her Book* (2000). She has won a number of literary prizes including the Commonwealth Prize for Best First Collection, the Forward Prize for Best Collection and the National Poetry Competition (twice). Her most recent collection is *Tender Taxes*, versions of Rilke's French poems (Faber, 2001).

Matthew Sweeney was born in Donegal in 1952 and has lived in London since 1973. He is one of the few Irish poets writing for both adults and children today. His collections for adults include *Cacti*, *The Bridal Suite* and *A Smell of Fish*. He has held various writing fellowships and won the Prudence Farmer Prize in 1984 and a Cholmondeley Award in 1987. His *Selected Poems* was published in 2002. His work for children includes *Up on the Roof: New and Selected Poems* (2001). He is editor of *The New Faber Book of Children's Poems*.

EMERGENCY KIT
Poems for Strange Times

edited by

JO SHAPCOTT *and* MATTHEW SWEENEY

faber and faber

First published in 1996
by Faber and Faber Limited
3 Queen Square London WCIN 3AU
This edition first published in 2004

Photoset by Wilmaset Ltd, Wirral
Printed in England by Mackays of Chatham plc, Chatham, Kent

This anthology © Jo Shapcott and Matthew Sweeney, 1996

Jo Shapcott and Matthew Sweeney are hereby identified as editors of this work in accordance with Section 77 of the Copyright, Designs and Patents Act 1988

A CIP record for this book
is available from the British Library

ISBN 0-571-22300-1

10 9 8 7 6 5 4 3 2 1

This strange century
With its slaughter of the innocent
Its flight to the moon –
CHARLES SIMIC, 'Street Scene'

Contents

Introduction, xv

Hamnavoe Market GEORGE MACKAY BROWN, 3
A Constable Calls SEAMUS HEANEY, 4
No MARK DOTY, 5
Red Roses ANNE SEXTON, 6
Harold's Walk GEOFFREY LEHMANN, 7
Owl GEORGE MACBETH, 10
A Bee PETER DIDSBURY, 11
The Heaven of Animals JAMES DICKEY, 12
Rat, O Rat ... CHRISTOPHER LOGUE, 13
My Rival's House LIZ LOCHHEAD, 14
A Doll's House KIT WRIGHT, 16
The Condom Tree CHASE TWICHELL, 17
Smoke SUSAN MITCHELL, 18
Listen Carefully PHILIP LEVINE, 20
'More Light! More Light!' ANTHONY HECHT, 21
I Am a Cameraman DOUGLAS DUNN, 22
Time Out MAURICE RIORDAN, 23
Mr and Mrs Scotland Are Dead KATHLEEN JAMIE, 26
Brief Lives OLIVE SENIOR, 27
Apple Island ROBERT GRAVES, 28
All Except Hannibal ROBERT GRAVES, 28
Palm Tree King JOHN AGARD, 29
Emergency Kit TANURE OJAIDE, 31
The Transposition of Clermont LES MURRAY, 32
Mercian Hymns IX, XII GEOFFREY HILL, 33
The Making of the Drum EDWARD KAMAU BRATHWAITE, 34
The Silent Piano LOUIS SIMPSON, 38
Bedtime Story GEORGE MACBETH, 38
The Horses EDWIN MUIR, 40
Johann Joachim Quantz's Five Lessons W. S. GRAHAM, 42
Variations for Two Pianos DONALD JUSTICE, 45
An American Roadside Elegy DAVE SMITH, 46

The Dream of Wearing Shorts Forever LES MURRAY, 47
Swineherd EILÉAN NÍ CHUILLEANÁIN, 50
Studying the Language EILÉAN NÍ CHUILLEANÁIN, 51
Diving into the Wreck ADRIENNE RICH, 51
Punishment SEAMUS HEANEY, 54
A Disused Shed in County Wexford DEREK MAHON, 56
The Bright Lights of Sarajevo TONY HARRISON, 58
Lightenings: viii SEAMUS HEANEY, 59
The Season of Phantasmal Peace DEREK WALCOTT, 60
From the Domain of Arnheim EDWIN MORGAN, 61
Ghetto MICHAEL LONGLEY, 62
Before SEAN O'BRIEN, 64
Swimming in the Flood JOHN BURNSIDE, 66
A Surprise in the Peninsula FLEUR ADCOCK, 67
The Visible Baby PETER REDGROVE, 68
Child Burial PAULA MEEHAN, 69
Cut SYLVIA PLATH, 70
Two Songs ADRIENNE RICH, 71
'O little one, this longing is the pits' MARILYN HACKER, 73
Ecstasy SHARON OLDS, 73
Coming HEATHER MCHUGH, 74
Spilt Milk SARAH MAGUIRE, 75
Maura THOMAS LYNCH, 76
Behold the Lilies of the Field ANTHONY HECHT, 77
Ye haue heard this yarn afore PETER READING, 79
Crusoe in England ELIZABETH BISHOP, 81
Moon Landing W. H. AUDEN, 86
Landing on the Moon ODIA OFEIMUN, 87
Outward LOUIS SIMPSON, 88
The Painter JOHN ASHBERY, 89
The Lost Pilot JAMES TATE, 90
Skywriting JAMIE GRANT, 92
Quiet Nights RAYMOND CARVER, 94
Lives DEREK MAHON, 94
The Red Judge D. M. BLACK, 96
The Video Box: 25 EDWIN MORGAN, 97

Lighthouse GERARD WOODWARD, 99
Popular Mechanics CHARLES SIMIC, 100
Always MARK STRAND, 101
I Am a Finn JAMES TATE, 102
I Am Still a Finn JAMES TATE, 103
Consolation TANURE OJAIDE, 104
The Turtle WILLIAM CARLOS WILLIAMS, 105
The Fish in the Stone RITA DOVE, 106
The Sea Eats the Land at Home
    GEORGE AWOONOR-WILLIAMS, 108
Meeting the British PAUL MULDOON, 109
In the Country of the Black Pig CHRISTOPHER HOPE, 109
Shame RICHARD WILBUR, 110
The Applicant SYLVIA PLATH, 111
Black March STEVIE SMITH, 113
Badly-Chosen Lover ROSEMARY TONKS, 114
Hydromaniac ROSEMARY TONKS, 115
My Shoes CHARLES SIMIC, 115
Dream Songs 4, 63 JOHN BERRYMAN, 116
Henry by Night JOHN BERRYMAN, 117
Memories of West Street and Lepke ROBERT LOWELL, 118
The Bight ELIZABETH BISHOP, 120
Boat Poem BERNARD SPENCER, 121
The Quality of Sprawl LES MURRAY, 123
The Monuments JOHN ASH, 125
A Low Temple ARUN KOLATKAR, 126
The Empty Church R. S. THOMAS, 127
The God of Love GEORGE MACBETH, 127
Fantasy of an African Boy JAMES BERRY, 129
The Ballad of the Shrieking Man JAMES FENTON, 130
A Grin TED HUGHES, 134
Not Like That ADRIENNE RICH, 135
A Dream of Hanging PATRICIA BEER, 137
Defying Gravity ROGER MCGOUGH, 138
Dance of the Cherry Blossom JACKIE KAY, 139
Death & Co. SYLVIA PLATH, 140

Warm to the Cuddly-toy Charm of a Koala Bear
  GAVIN EWART, 141
Dream of a Slave GAVIN EWART, 142
Song PETER REDGROVE, 143
Hitcher SIMON ARMITAGE, 144
Species CHARLES BOYLE, 145
Dreaming in the Shanghai Restaurant D. J. ENRIGHT, 146
A Consumer's Report PETER PORTER, 147
When a Beautiful Woman Gets on the Jutiapa Bus
  BELLE WARING, 148
Being a Wife SELIMA HILL, 149
Against Coupling FLEUR ADCOCK, 150
The Ecstasy of St Saviour's Avenue NEIL ROLLINSON, 151
The Sheep Child JAMES DICKEY, 152
The Geranium THEODORE ROETHKE, 154
Grimalkin THOMAS LYNCH, 155
Before You Cut Loose, SIMON ARMITAGE, 157
The Strange Case MICHAEL ONDAATJE, 158
Country Fair CHARLES SIMIC, 159
Dancing in Vacationland STEPHEN DOBYNS, 159
1668 DOM MORAES, 161
Austerities CHARLES SIMIC, 162
Nigger Sweat EDWARD BAUGH, 163
The Emigrant Irish EAVAN BOLAND, 164
The Woman on the Dump ELIZABETH SPIRES, 165
The Man Who Invented Pain CRAIG RAINE, 166
'now is a ship' E.E. CUMMINGS, 169
The Italians Are Excited FREDA DOWNIE, 169
The Railway Station ARUN KOLATKAR, 170
Sleeping Compartment NORMAN MACCAIG, 173
The Taxis LOUIS MACNEICE, 174
A Sign Illuminated ROY FISHER, 175
Death of a Farmyard GEOFFREY GRIGSON, 176
The Explosion PHILIP LARKIN, 176
Timer TONY HARRISON, 177
The Scissors Ceremony MICHAEL LONGLEY, 178

The Plain Sense of Things WALLACE STEVENS, 179
Where Are the Waters of Childhood? MARK STRAND, 179
My Mother's Lips C. K. WILLIAMS, 181
Calvin Klein's *Obsession* CIARAN CARSON, 183
A Private Bottling DON PATERSON, 187
Another Woman IMTIAZ DHARKER, 190
Adultery CAROL ANN DUFFY, 192
This Dead Relationship KATHERINE PIERPOINT, 193
Routine Day Sonnet A. K. RAMANUJAN, 195
Raymond of the Rooftops PAUL DURCAN, 196
From a Conversation During Divorce CAROL RUMENS, 197
Onions WILLIAM MATTHEWS, 198
Oatmeal GALWAY KINNELL, 199
When I Grow Up HUGO WILLIAMS, 202
Rat Jelly MICHAEL ONDAATJE, 203
Out West BILL MANHIRE, 204
As It Should Be DEREK MAHON, 204
Script Conference JOHN HARTLEY WILLIAMS, 205
Aisle of Dogs CHASE TWICHELL, 207
On the Venom Farm RUTH PADEL, 208
The Sting TOM PAULIN, 210
Raptor R. S. THOMAS, 212
From the Childhood of Jesus ROBERT PINSKY, 213
You Will Know When You Get There ALLEN CURNOW, 215
Caliban's Books MICHAEL DONAGHY, 216
The Draft Horse ROBERT FROST, 217
Why Brownlee Left PAUL MULDOON, 217
Street EILÉAN NÍ CHUILLEANÁIN, 218
The Other TED HUGHES, 218
Not Waving but Drowning STEVIE SMITH, 219
Skunk Hour ROBERT LOWELL, 220
The Old Fools PHILIP LARKIN, 222
I Go Back to May 1937 SHARON OLDS, 223
You Hated Spain TED HUGHES, 224
An October Salmon TED HUGHES, 225
Notations of Ten Summer Minutes NORMAN MACCAIG, 228

Soap Suds LOUIS MACNEICE, 228
A Sofa in the Forties SEAMUS HEANEY, 229
Ancient Evenings MICHAEL HOFMANN, 231
My Second Marriage to My First Husband ALICE FULTON, 232
Lily Pond VICKI FEAVER, 233
Houdini MONIZA ALVI, 234
In Your Mind CAROL ANN DUFFY, 235
Love from a Foreign City LAVINIA GREENLAW, 236
The Letter ANDREW MOTION, 237
Looking Up SUJATA BHATT, 238
Knot SUSAN WICKS, 239
Small Female Skull CAROL ANN DUFFY, 240
Green Sees Things in Waves AUGUST KLEINZAHLER, 241
Two Hangovers JAMES WRIGHT, 242
Death of a Poet CHARLES CAUSLEY, 243
Memento Mori BILLY COLLINS, 244
Death of an Irishwoman MICHAEL HARTNETT, 245
Cups GWEN HARWOOD, 246
Hospital Evening GWEN HARWOOD, 246
The Hospital PATRICK KAVANAGH, 247
The Tune the Old Cow Died of NORMAN NICHOLSON, 248
What Work Is PHILIP LEVINE, 249
The Patriot NISSIM EZEKIEL, 251
The Second Voyage EILÉAN NÍ CHUILLEANÁIN, 252
The Sea E. A. MARKHAM, 254
The Birth PAUL MULDOON, 254
Balloons SYLVIA PLATH, 255
The King of the Cats Is Dead PETER PORTER, 256
The Broad Bean Sermon LES MURRAY, 257
Homecoming BRUCE DAWE, 259
Fifteen Million Plastic Bags ADRIAN MITCHELL, 260
Presidents MICHAEL HEFFERNAN, 261
Portraits of Tudor Statesmen U. A. FANTHORPE, 262
Not My Best Side U. A. FANTHORPE, 262
My Belovèd Compares Herself to a Pint of Stout
        PAUL DURCAN, 264

Margin Prayer from an Ancient Psalter IAN DUHIG, 265
The Lion for Real ALLEN GINSBERG, 267
Underwear LAWRENCE FERLINGHETTI, 269
Black Silk TESS GALLAGHER, 272
A True Account of Talking to the Sun at Fire Island
    FRANK O'HARA, 273
Prayer HUGO WILLIAMS, 275
A Priest in the Sabbath Dawn Addresses His Somnolent Mistress
    PETER DIDSBURY, 276
Stealing CAROL ANN DUFFY, 277
The Congress of the Insomniacs CHARLES SIMIC, 278
Mama Dot Learns to Fly FRED D'AGUIAR, 279
Seeing Off a Friend STEPHEN DOBYNS, 279
What the Doctor Said RAYMOND CARVER, 280
The Trees ADRIENNE RICH, 281
For and Against the Environment D. M. BLACK, 282
Not Being Oedipus JOHN HEATH-STUBBS, 285
Water PHILIP LARKIN, 286
Naked Vision GWEN HARWOOD, 287
Finale JUDITH WRIGHT, 287
The Big Words BRENDAN KENNELLY, 288
The Tough Guy of London KOJO GYINYE KYEI, 290
Depressed by a Book of Bad Poetry, I Walk Toward an Unused
Pasture and Invite the Insects to Join ME
JAMES WRIGHT, 290
The Beast in the Space W. S. GRAHAM, 291
What the Chairman Told Tom BASIL BUNTING, 292

Acknowledgements, 295
Index of Poets, 303

Introduction

In the spring of 1989, the two of us met every week in London to run simultaneous poetry classes for adults. We would bring in what we liked to think of as bootleg books – books at that time published only in America – and read from them, often to the astonishment and pleasure of our students, who had never heard poems quite like these. Among the poets whose work we introduced were Stephen Dobyns, Sharon Olds, Mark Strand and Charles Simic, as well as some of their better-known progenitors: Elizabeth Bishop, Sylvia Plath, Miroslav Holub, Pablo Neruda. We didn't limit our readings to the classes, nor even to sessions in the bar afterwards. In one of our groups there was a blind student, who travelled home on the underground in the same direction as we did, and we couldn't resist reading some favourites out loud to him there and then. What we did not anticipate was the response of our fellow passengers: laughter, applause – and surprise that poetry could be like that.

Emergency Kit reflects our continuing interest in writing of this sort: poetry which strikes from new and surprising angles, proposes unconventional connections, or takes on extraordinary subject matter; poetry, in other words, which fulfils Robert Frost's demand that it should be 'a fresh look and a fresh listen'. This is the poetry which seems to us to have responded most aptly and inventively to the closing stages of 'this strange century', as well as offering what could be the most hopeful approach to the next one.

So you will find in this book poems which discover the folklore and fables of our time in the territory of urban myth, or, conversely, bring the light of ancient myth to bear on the problems of our own day. There are others which present wild, childlike tales whose distorting vision breaks through to the truth; which make risky journeys into the unconscious and back; which revel in a rowdy irreverence or an odd eroticism; which are simultaneously hilarious and grim; or which appear to contain whole new worlds, parallel universes.

When we were first asked to put this anthology together, our idea was simply to collect the poems of our time which had most excited us in this way. It soon became clear, though, that such poetry had not sprung from nowhere and that, to make better sense of the foreground, we had to look at what lay behind it. Choosing the mid-1950s as our starting point allowed us to see how the generations immediately preceding our own had pointed the way. Among those who seemed to us to have been influential were not only figures of accepted stature like Sylvia Plath, Frank O'Hara, William Carlos Williams, Wallace Stevens and Stevie Smith, but also a few like W. S. Graham or Rosemary Tonks whose impact, though less widely noticed, is still important. Others who came later but who are now often overlooked – such as George MacBeth and D. M. Black – have exerted their own distinct influence. Beyond that, the wider time-span of roughly forty years enabled us to include the work of poets who, while not normally associated with the territory defined here, have all made incursions into it: Robert Frost, Robert Lowell, John Berryman, Elizabeth Bishop, W. H. Auden, Adrienne Rich, Edwin Muir, E. E. Cummings, Louis MacNeice, Basil Bunting, Philip Larkin, James Wright, Lawrence Ferlinghetti, Allen Ginsberg, Derek Walcott, Ted Hughes, Seamus Heaney, Edward Kamau Brathwaite, Les Murray and Gwen Harwood.

Our contents list is an international one, with some of the finest poets of our day gracing it. But the point was never simply to assemble the big names; nor have we set out to match the size of any poet's reputation with an equivalent showing in these pages. This is a poem-oriented book, not a poets' league table like some recent anthologies. As well as earning inclusion by their merits, poems had to fit generically. For this reason, many of our own favourites have not found a place.

We also made an early decision to limit our attention to poems written in English. This was purely from considerations of size. In fact, our book shares an imaginative landscape with the work of poets writing in a number of other languages. The Czech Miroslav Holub, the Serbian Vasco Popa, the Mexican Octavio Paz and the Chilean Pablo Neruda come immediately to mind; and it's surely no coincidence that in 1975 Charles Simic – himself a Serbian by birth – and fellow-American Mark Strand edited an anthology, *Another Republic*, designed to introduce North American readers to the poetry of Europe and South America which had exerted such an influence on their own generation, members of which now appear in *Emergency Kit*.

The poetry of these parts of the world was often written under oppression, its oblique, riddling and parable-like procedures allowing it to say things the censor couldn't pick up. The effect of the best of this writing had been so direct and profound – thanks not just to *Another Republic*, but to the series of Penguin Modern European Poets which flourished briefly in the 1970s and to the pioneering volumes published by smaller presses on both sides of the Atlantic – that many English-language poets of the period under consideration have either consciously or unconsciously absorbed it. As a result, their work has gained a subversiveness, a humour, a gift for exaggeration and an imagistic power that can change the very way you look at the world.

But why the need for such writing now? We live in an age when scientists can see inside every cell in the body and are learning more and more, through space exploration and the advances of astrophysics (Voyager, the Hubble telescope, for example), about the outer reaches of the universe and the distant history of life itself. It occurs to us that, just as Donne and Marvell were compelled by the discoveries of their time, so the poets in this book are responding to or reflecting the surprises of ours.

TV, tabloids, movies, virtual reality, the Internet – all these have encouraged us to take the extraordinary for granted. We have watched men walk on the moon, we talk to each other across space and time, we conduct our business and our courtships on the 'net'. Isn't it inevitable, then, that these days poetry should be written which makes free with the boundaries of realism, crossing this way and that, at will?

In a recent interview, Seamus Heaney said: 'I admire works that use fantasy, treat the world as a trampoline.' We admire them too, and many poems in *Emergency Kit* fit that description.

But however far and freely they travel, they always come back to the world we wake up to, illuminating, from whatever angle, our day-to-day concerns. Other poems in the book may be more ostensibly realist in manner, with their focus on the actual and the ordinary, but even here there is always a glint of what Elizabeth Bishop called 'the surrealism of everyday life'.

It is important to mention that we are not talking about an entirely new phenomenon. Antecedents may be found as far back as you like: in folklore, fable and mythology, anywhere, anytime; in the hyperbole of medieval Irish poetry; in Old English riddles and Chaucer's speaking animals; in Spenser's lush, allegorical fantasies; in the idiosyncrasies of Smart, Blake and Dickinson; in Coleridge and other nineteenth-century exponents of the Gothic; in Swift, Sterne, Dickens, Gogol, Melville, Kafka, Flann O'Brien and Beckett. And in our time this vein has been widely acknowledged and appreciated, often under the heading of 'magical realism', in the prose fiction of Gabriel García Marquez, Jorge Luis Borges, Angela Carter, Isabel Allende, Italo Calvino, Jeanette Winterson and Günter Grass. Even so, there has been a strange reluctance to recognize that poetry in English can, does or should operate in similar territory, a few celebrated and supposedly isolated cases notwithstanding – Britain's so-called 'Martian School', for instance. *Emergency Kit* shows that this tendency is not so exceptional. The selection of poems itself is designed to surprise by bringing to light connections and family resemblances not previously identified.

What follows is intended not for specialists but for everybody. The clarity of the poems included should ensure that new readers – young readers and writers, especially – will be inspired by the imaginative risks taken. This is the anthology we wish we could have read when we were starting out: a book that demonstrates how poetry can be fun and a serious matter at the same time; can crack the world open and put it together again in new and convincing ways.

Jo Shapcott and Matthew Sweeney
London, 1996

Emergency Kit

Hamnavoe Market

They drove to the Market with ringing pockets.

Folster found a girl
Who put lipstick wounds on his face and throat,
Small and diagonal, like red doves.

Johnston stood beside the barrel.
All day he stood there.
He woke in a ditch, his mouth full of ashes.

Grieve bought a balloon and a goldfish.
He swung through the air.
He fired shotguns, rolled pennies, ate sweet fog from a stick.

Heddle was at the Market also.
I know nothing of his activities.
He is and always was a quiet man.

Garson went three rounds with a negro boxer,
And received thirty shillings,
Much applause, and an eye loaded with thunder.

Where did they find Flett?
They found him in a brazen circle,
All flame and blood, a new Salvationist.

A gypsy saw in the hand of Halcro
Great strolling herds, harvests, a proud woman.
He wintered in the poorhouse.

They drove home from the Market under the stars
Except for Johnston
Who lay in a ditch, his mouth full of dying fires.

GEORGE MACKAY BROWN

A Constable Calls

His bicycle stood at the window-sill,
The rubber cowl of a mud-splasher
Skirting the front mudguard,
Its fat black handlegrips

Heating in sunlight, the 'spud'
Of the dynamo gleaming and cocked back,
The pedal treads hanging relieved
Of the boot of the law.

His cap was upside down
On the floor, next his chair.
The line of its pressure ran like a bevel
In his slightly sweating hair.

He had unstrapped
The heavy ledger, and my father
Was making tillage returns
In acres, roods, and perches.

Arithmetic and fear.
I sat staring at the polished holster
With its buttoned flap, the braid cord
Looped into the revolver butt.

'Any other root crops?
Mangolds? Marrowstems? Anything like that?'
'No.' But was there not a line
Of turnips where the seed ran out

In the potato field? I assumed
Small guilts and sat
Imagining the black hole in the barracks.
He stood up, shifted the baton-case

Further round on his belt,
Closed the domesday book,

Fitted his cap back with two hands,
And looked at me as he said goodbye.

A shadow bobbed in the window.
He was snapping the carrier spring
Over the ledger. His boot pushed off
And the bicycle ticked, ticked, ticked.

SEAMUS HEANEY

No

The children have brought their wood turtle
into the dining hall
because they want us to feel

the power they have
when they hold a house
in their own hands, want us to feel

alien lacquer and the little thrill
that he might, like God, show his face.
He's the color of ruined wallpaper,

of cognac, and he's closed,
pulled in as though he'll never come out;
nothing shows but the plummy leather

of the legs, his claws resembling clusters
of diminutive raspberries.
They know he makes night

anytime he wants, so perhaps
he feels at the center of everything,
as they do. His age,

greater than that of anyone
around the table, is a room
from which they are excluded,

though they don't mind,
since they can carry this perfect
building anywhere. They love

that he might poke out
his old, old face, but doesn't.
I think the children smell unopened,

like unlit candles, as they heft him
around the table, praise his secrecy,
holding to each adult face

his prayer,
the single word of the shell,
which is no.

MARK DOTY

Red Roses

Tommy is three and when he's bad
his mother dances with him.
She puts on the record,
'Red Roses for a Blue Lady'
and throws him across the room.
Mind you,
she never laid a hand on him,
only the wall laid a hand on him.
He gets red roses in different places,
the head, that time he was as sleepy as a river,
the back, that time he was a broken scarecrow,
the arm like a diamond had bitten it,
the leg, twisted like a licorice stick,
all the dance they did together,
Blue Lady and Tommy.
You fell, she said, just remember you fell.
I fell, is all he told the doctors

in the big hospital. A nice lady came
and asked him questions but because
he didn't want to be sent away he said, I fell.
He never said anything else although he could talk fine.
He never told about the music
or how she'd sing and shout
holding him up and throwing him.

He pretends he is her ball.
He tries to fold up and bounce
but he squashes like fruit.
For he loves Blue Lady and the spots
of red red roses he gives her.

ANNE SEXTON

Harold's Walk

He turned and waved.
He was one year and a month.
With cobweb-light hair,
the colour of leatherwood honey,
brown poet's eyes
and refined cheekbones
burnished red like the blush
on a white Shanghai peach,
he turned and waved.
There was a graze on his left nostril,
a thin scab in the fold where it met the cheek.
He was wearing a white singlet
and plastic pilchers.
Having farewelled us
he headed off down the road
like a tottering upright tortoise.
Propelled by an unstoppable business,
his pink feet imprinted the hot soft dust

of the road that led
into that Old Testament afternoon,
the biblical vastness of southwest Queensland.

He escaped as we were placing
a small native pine in the back of the utility.
A single blow of the axe, a sharp smell of resin
and we had a Christmas tree.

But Christmas and tomorrow had no meaning for him.
His sole interest
was the random stagger of his short fat legs
and this curious ability
to distance himself from objects.

No birds or insects
announced their presence in the heavy stillness
as water and life withdrew.
The rapid and twittering dialects
of finches and wagtails, the warbling of magpies
that had made the morning into a watermeadow
of sounds and activity
were a hypothesis cancelled in the oven air
by the axeblade of sunlight.
There were no geckoes, whose ghostlike transparent bodies
attracted by insect harvests
frolicked on flywire screens at night.
They too were hiding.

But the child, an escaping particle, whose energy
had no objective,
who woke and could not be contained,
small fists hoisting the face up to look
over cot-bars
and grab for the horizon,
ran tottering and uncompromised through hot dust.
If we had tried to stop him
he would have squealed, 'No, no,'

one of his three words—
the others 'oh' for surprise
and 'mamy' for need and distress.
He ran with no sense of history
through brigalow country unreformed like himself,
that was cleared long ago with crowbar, axe and shovel,
cleared again by bulldozer and chains,
and cleared once more
by a blade cutting beneath the surface.

But the seeds and roots are unrepentant
as the tortoise-child
who runs with no fear of marks in the road
that may lead to a death-adder
in a camouflaged coil of dust.

His momentum was unadulterated by knowledge.
His hypothesis rejected our evidence.
He ran falling on his plastic pilchers
and picking himself up,
unwilling to learn
except what he could teach himself
from placing stones in his mouth
and tearing leaves apart with his fingers.

The night sky above brigalow country
is a Joseph's coat of stars,
but if your finger tracked the Southern Cross
or saucepan for him,
he grabbed at the finger and not the stars.
Because there was hot available air
into which he could run, he ran.
Balancing himself with arms apart
his stops and starts were unpredictable.
The play of free will—
liberated by chaos from classical physics.

The wild purple verbena scrambling by the road,
milk thistles,
and grasses bending with the weight of seeds
were the instantly touchable aromatic kingdom
through which he tottered,
startled only by the grasshopper's sudden parachute
of lemon splashed with a blood drop.
Some hundreds of yards further on
he turned and waved again
a last farewell
from eyes set in an oval whimsical head,
before entering his chosen land
of wilga and blue native pine.

GEOFFREY LEHMANN

Owl

is my favourite. Who flies
like a nothing through the night,
who-whoing. Is a feather
duster in leafy corners ring-a-rosy-ing
boles of mice. Twice

you hear him call. Who
is he looking for? You hear
him hoovering over the floor
of the wood. O would you be gold
rings in the driving skull

if you could? Hooded and
vulnerable by the winter suns
owl looks. Is the grain of bark
in the dark. Round beaks are at
work in the pellety nest,

resting. Owl is an eye
in the barn. For a hole
in the trunk owl's blood
is to blame. Black talons in the
petrified fur! Cold walnut hands

on the case of the brain! In the reign
of the chicken owl comes like
a god. Is a goad in
the rain to the pink eyes,
dripping. For a meal in the day

flew, killed, on the moor. Six
mouths are the seed of his
arc in the season. Torn meat
from the sky. Owl lives
by the claws of his brain. On the branch

in the sever of the hand's
twigs owl is a backward look.
Flown wind in the skin. Fine
rain in the bones. Owl breaks
like the day. Am an owl, am an owl.

GEORGE MACBETH

A Bee

Become at last a bee
I took myself naked to town,
with plastic sacks of yellow turmeric
taped to my wizened thighs.

I'd been buying it for weeks,
along with foods I no longer had a need for,
in small amounts from every corner grocer,
so as not to arouse their suspicion.

It was hard, running and buzzing,
doing the bee-dance. I ached
at the roots of my wings, and hardly yet discerned
that I flew towards reparation,
that in my beehood my healing had been commenced.

Words they use in this hive. To me it seems still
that clumps of tall blue flowers,
which smiled as they encroached,
had been born of my apian will,
in which to my shame I struggled for a moment,
and stained the air with clouds of my dearly bought gold.

PETER DIDSBURY

The Heaven of Animals

Here they are. The soft eyes open.
If they have lived in a wood
It is a wood.
If they have lived on plains
It is grass rolling
Under their feet forever.

Having no souls, they have come,
Anyway, beyond their knowing.
Their instincts wholly bloom
And they rise.
The soft eyes open.

To match them, the landscape flowers,
Outdoing, desperately
Outdoing what is required:
The richest wood,
The deepest field.

For some of these,
It could not be the place
It is, without blood.
These hunt, as they have done,
But with claws and teeth grown perfect,

More deadly than they can believe.
They stalk more silently,
And crouch on the limbs of trees,
And their descent
Upon the bright backs of their prey

May take years
In a sovereign floating of joy.
And those that are hunted
Know this as their life,
Their reward: to walk

Under such trees in full knowledge
Of what is in glory above them,
And to feel no fear,
But acceptance, compliance.
Fulfilling themselves without pain

At the cycle's center,
They tremble, they walk
Under the tree,
They fall, they are torn,
They rise, they walk again.

JAMES DICKEY

Rat, O Rat...

never in all my life have I seen
as handsome a rat as you.
Thank you for noticing my potatoes.

O Rat, I am not rich.
I left you a note concerning potatoes,
but I see that I placed it too high
and you could not read it.

O Rat, my wife and I are cursed
with the possession of a large and hungry dog;
it worries us that he might learn your name —
which is forever on our lips.

O Rat, consider my neighbour:
he has eight children (all of them older
and more intelligent than mine)
and if you lived in his house, Rat,

ten good Christians
(if we include his wife)
would sing your praises nightly,
whereas in my house there are only five.

CHRISTOPHER LOGUE

My Rival's House

is peopled with many surfaces.
Ormolu and gilt, slipper satin,
lush velvet couches,
cushions so stiff you can't sink in.
Tables polished clear enough to see distortions in.

We take our shoes off at her door,
shuffle stocking-soled, tiptoe – the parquet floor
is beautiful and its surface must
be protected. Dust
cover, drawn shade,
won't let the surface colour fade.

Silver sugar-tongs and silver salver
my rival serves us tea.
She glosses over him and me.
I am all edges, a surface, a shell
and yet my rival thinks she means me well.
But what squirms beneath her surface I can tell.
Soon, my rival
capped tooth, polished nail
will fight, fight foul for her survival.
Deferential, daughterly, I sip
and thank her nicely for each bitter cup.

And I have much to thank her for.
This son she bore –
first blood to her –
never, never can escape scot free
the sour potluck of family.
And oh how close
this family that furnishes my rival's place.

Lady of the house.
Queen bee.

She is far more unconscious,
far more dangerous than me.
Listen, I was always my own worst enemy.
She has taken even this from me.

She dishes up her dreams for breakfast.
Dinner, and her salt tears pepper our soup.
She won't
give up.

LIZ LOCHHEAD

[15]

A Doll's House

A man sat staring at a doll's house
Hour after hour and more and more
He believed. He could see
In the kitchenette two personettes
And one of them was standing in the sink
And one lay on the floor.

The man stared more and more.

The bed in the bathroom was neatly made up with a
Pink eiderdown neatly made up from a
Pink ribbon. But no one was in the bed
And no one was in the bathroom.
Only a horse
Was trying the door.

The man stared more and more.

Then softly the man went in,
Edged down
Past the creaky banisters, down
He crept
To the hall, hid nimbly
Behind a cow.

From the sink: 'My dear,
That tractor's on the roof again, I fear.'
Sadly from the floor: 'These nights
It seems to be always there.'

Then silence between
Personette A and Personette B,
Now like a matchstick drumming a plastic thimble,
Now like the sea.

From the sink: 'How I wish, my dear,
That you and I could move house.

But these matters are not in our hands. Our directives
Come from above.'
Said the floor: 'How can we ever move house
When the house keeps moving, my love?'

A man sat staring at a doll's house
Hour after hour and more and more
He believed he could see
Perspectives of the terrorized world,
Delicate, as a new-tooled body,
Monstrous, mad as he.

KIT WRIGHT

The Condom Tree

Pleasure must slip
right through memory's barbed wire,
because sex makes lost things reappear.
This afternoon when I shut my eyes
beneath his body's heavy braille,
I fell through the rosy darkness
all the way back to my tenth year,
the year of the secret
place by the river,
where the old dam spilled
long ropes of water and the froth
chafed the small stones smooth.
I looked up and there it was,
a young maple
still raw in early spring,
and drooping pale
from every reachable branch
dozens of latex blooms.
I knew what they were,
that the older kids

had hung them there,
but the tree – was it beautiful,
caught in that dirty floral light,
or was it an ugly thing?
Beautiful first, and ugly afterward,
when I saw up close
the shriveled human skins?
That must be right,
though in the remembering
its value has been changed again,
and now that flowering
dapples the two of us
with its tendered shadows,
dapples the rumpled bed as it slips
out of the damp present
into our separate pasts.

CHASE TWICHELL

Smoke

At night the child takes down
the helmet and puts it on, the bullet hole
facing front. It does this in secret,
standing on the bed

to make itself bigger,
a dark figure confronting the mirror. God knows
who the helmet belonged to, the father
brought it back from a war

along with the gun which the child
plays with now that the firing pin's removed.
The mother hates the helmet with its leather
chin strap and hides it

in the closet. The child
wants to drink the shadows at the bottom
where a man lived, where he put his hair and brains
and kept his cigarettes.

No one likes the child
to point the gun at them. The child asks,
Did you kill anyone? pointing
the gun at the father,

and frankly, is disappointed
by the answer. The mirror does not disappoint
the child. At night it fills with shadows and barbed
wire and the dead soldier

who comes to talk in German,
which the child does not understand, saying
only *Ja, ja.* The soldier is careful
to stand on his side

of the mirror. Sometimes
the child steals a cigarette from the mother's
bag, but the soldier prefers his own. So,
the child lights up for itself,

taking a long drag
as it lies back in bed, the lighted end
all that's visible in the dark.
It is strange to think

when the child grows up
this is how she will look after making
love, holding the smoke in her mouth
as if it were precious.

SUSAN MITCHELL

Listen Carefully

My sister rises from our bed hours before dawn.
I smell her first cigarette and fall back asleep
until she sits on the foot of the bed to pull
on her boots. I shouldn't look, but I do,
knowing she's still naked from the waist up.
She sees me looking and smiles, musses my hair,
whispers something secret into my ear, something
I can't tell anyone because it makes no sense.
Hours later I waken in an empty room
smelling of no yesterdays. The sunlight streams
across the foot of the bed, and for a moment
I actually think it's Saturday, and I'm free.
Let me be frank about this: my older sister
is not smart. I answer all her mail for her,
and on Sundays I even make dinner because
the one cookbook confuses her, although
it claims to be the way to a man's heart.
She wants to learn the way, she wants
a husband, she tells me, but at twenty-six she's
beginning to wonder. She makes good money
doing piece work, assembling the cups that cap
the four ends of a cross of a universal joint.
I've seen her at work, her face cut with slashes
of grease while with tweezers she positions
the tiny rods faster than you or I could ever,
her eyes fixed behind goggles, her mind God
knows where, roaming over all the errors
she thinks make her life. She doesn't know why
her men aren't good to her. I've rubbed
hand cream into the bruises on her shoulders,
I've seen what they've done, I've even cried
along with her. By now I believe I know
exactly what you're thinking. Although I don't
get home until after one, we sleep

in the same bed every night, unless she's
not home. If you're thinking there's no way
we wouldn't be driven to each other, no way
we could resist, no way someone as wronged
as my beautiful sister could have a choice
about something so basic, then you're
the one who's wrong. You haven't heard a word.

PHILIP LEVINE

'More Light! More Light!'

for Heinrich Blücher and Hannah Arendt

Composed in the Tower before his execution
These moving verses, and being brought at that time
Painfully to the stake, submitted, declaring thus:
'I implore my God to witness that I have made no crime.'

Nor was he forsaken of courage, but the death was horrible,
The sack of gunpowder failing to ignite.
His legs were blistered sticks on which the black sap
Bubbled and burst as he howled for the Kindly Light.

And that was but one, and by no means one of the worst;
Permitted at least his pitiful dignity;
And such as were by made prayers in the name of Christ,
That shall judge all men, for his soul's tranquillity.

We move now to outside a German wood.
Three men are there commanded to dig a hole
In which the two Jews are ordered to lie down
And be buried alive by the third, who is a Pole.

Not light from the shrine at Weimar beyond the hill
Nor light from heaven appeared. But he did refuse.
A Lüger settled back deeply in its glove.
He was ordered to change places with the Jews.

Much casual death had drained away their souls.
The thick dirt mounted toward the quivering chin.
When only the head was exposed the order came
To dig him out again and to get back in.

No light, no light in the blue Polish eye.
When he finished a riding boot packed down the earth.
The Lüger hovered lightly in its glove.
He was shot in the belly and in three hours bled to death.

No prayers or incense rose up in those hours
Which grew to be years, and every day came mute
Ghosts from the ovens, sifting through crisp air,
And settled upon his eyes in a black soot.

ANTHONY HECHT

I Am a Cameraman

They suffer, and I catch only the surface.
The rest is inexpressible, beyond
What can be recorded. You can't be them.
If they'd talk to you, you might guess
What pain is like though they might spit on you.

Film is just a reflection
Of the matchless despair of the century.
There have been twenty centuries since charity began.
Indignation is day-to-day stuff;
It keeps us off the streets, it keeps us watching.

Film has no words of its own.
It is a silent waste of things happening
Without us, when it is too late to help.
What of the dignity of those caught suffering?
It hurts me. I robbed them of privacy.

My young friends think Film will be all of Art.
It will be revolutionary proof.
Their films will not guess wrongly and will not lie.
They'll film what is happening behind barbed wire.
They'll always know the truth and be famous.

Politics softens everything.
Truth is known only to its victims.
All else is photographs – a documentary
The starving and the playboys perish in.
Life disguises itself with professionalism.

Life tells the biggest lies of all,
And draws wages from itself.
Truth is a landscape the saintly tribes live on,
And all the lenses of Japan and Germany
Wouldn't know how to focus on it.

Life flickers on the frame like beautiful hummingbirds.
That is the film that always comes out blank.
The painting the artist can't get shapes to fit.
The poem that shrugs off every word you try.
The music no one has ever heard.

DOUGLAS DUNN

Time Out

Such is modern life   STEPHEN DOBYNS

The two young ones fed, bathed, zippered, read to and sung to.
   Asleep.
Time now to stretch on the sofa. Time for a cigarette.
When he realizes he's out. Clean out of smokes.
He grabs a fistful of coins, hesitates to listen before
Pulling the door softly to. Then sprints for the cornershop.

When he trips on a shoelace, head first into the path of a U-
    turning cab.
The screech of brakes is coterminous with his scream.
The Somalian shopkeeper, who summons the ambulance,
    knows the face,
But the name or address? No – just someone he remembers
Popping in, always with kids (this he doesn't say).

Casualty is at full stretch and the white thirtyish male,
Unshaven, with broken runners, is going nowhere. Is cleanly
    dead.
Around midnight an orderly rummages his pockets: £2.50 in
    change,
A latchkey, two chestnuts, one mitten, scraps of paper,
Some written on, but no wallet, cards, licence, or address
    book.

Around 2 a.m. he's put on ice, with a numbered tag.
Around 3 a.m. a child wakes, cries, then wails for attention.
But after ten minutes, unusually, goes back to sleep.
Unusually his twin sleeps on undisturbed till six o'clock,
When they both wake together, kicking, calling out *dada, dada*

Happily: well slept, still dry, crooning and pretend-reading in
    the half-light.
Then one slides to the floor, toddles to the master bedroom
And, seeing the empty (unmade) bed, toddles towards the
    stairs,
Now followed by the other, less stable, who stumbles halfway
    down
And both roll the last five steps to the bottom, screaming.

To be distracted by the post plopping onto the mat: all junk,
Therefore bulky, colourful, glossy, illicit. Time slips.
Nine o'clock: hungry, soiled, sensing oddness and absence,
Edgy together and whimpering now, when they discover the
    TV
Still on, its 17-channel console alive to their touch.

The Italian Parliament, sumo wrestling, the Austrian Grand
    Prix,
Opera, the Parcel Force ad, see them through to half past nine
When distress takes hold and the solid stereophonic screaming
    begins,
Relentless and shrill enough to penetrate the attention
Of the retired French pharmacist next door

Who at, say ten o'clock, pokes a broomstick through her rear
    window
To rattle theirs: magical silencing effect, lasting just so long
As it takes for the elderly woman to draw up her shopping list,
To retrieve two tenners from the ice-compartment, dead-lock
    her front doors,
Shake her head at the sunning milk, and make it to the bus.

Let us jump then to 10 p.m., to the nightmare dénouement...
No, let us duck right now out of this story, for such it is:
An idle, day-bed, Hitchcockian fantasy (though prompted by a
    news item,
A clockwork scenario: it was five days before that three-year-
    old
Was discovered beside the corpse of his Irish dad in Northolt).

Let us get *this* dad in and out of the shop, safely across the
    street,
Safely indoors again, less a couple of quid, plus the listings
    mags
And ten Silk Cut, back on board the sofa: reprieved, released,
    relaxed,
Thinking it's time for new sneakers, for a beard trim, for an
    overall
Rethink in the hair department. Time maybe to move on from
    the fags.

MAURICE RIORDAN

Mr and Mrs Scotland Are Dead

On the civic amenity landfill site,
the coup, the dump beyond the cemetery
and the 30-mile-an-hour sign, her stiff
old ladies' bags, open mouthed, spew
postcards sent from small Scots towns
in 1960: Peebles, Largs, the rock-gardens
of Carnoustie, tinted in the dirt.
Mr and Mrs Scotland, here is the hand you were dealt:
fair but cool, showery but nevertheless,
Jean asks kindly; the lovely scenery;
in careful school-room script –
The Beltane Queen was crowned today.
But Mr and Mrs Scotland are dead.

Couldn't he have burned them? Released
in a grey curl of smoke
this pattern for a cable knit? Or this:
tossed between a toppled fridge
and sweet-stinking anorak: *Dictionary for Mothers*
M:– Milk, *the woman who worries . . .*;
And here, Mr Scotland's John Bull Puncture Repair Kit;
those days when he knew intimately
the thin roads of his country, hedgerows
hanged with small black brambles' hearts;
and here, for God's sake, his last few joiners' tools,
SCOTLAND, SCOTLAND, stamped on their tired handles.

Do we take them? Before the bulldozer comes
to make more room, to shove aside
his shaving brush, her button tin.
Do we save this toolbox, these old-fashioned views
addressed, after all, to Mr and Mrs Scotland?
Should we reach and take them? And then?
Forget them, till that person enters
our silent house, begins to open

to the light our kitchen drawers,
and performs for us this perfunctory rite:
the sweeping up, the turning out.

KATHLEEN JAMIE

Brief Lives

Gardening in the Tropics, you never know
what you'll turn up. Quite often, bones.
In some places they say when volcanoes
erupt, they spew out dense and monumental
as stones the skulls of *desaparecidos*
– the disappeared ones. Mine is only
a kitchen garden so I unearth just
occasional skeletons. The latest
was of a young man from the country who
lost his way and crossed the invisible
boundary into rival political territory.
I buried him again so he can carry on
growing. Our cemeteries are thriving too.
The newest addition was the drug baron
wiped out in territorial competition
who had this stunning funeral
complete with twenty-one-gun salute
and attended by everyone, especially
the young girls famed for the vivacity
of their dress, their short skirts and
even briefer lives.

OLIVE SENIOR

Apple Island

Though cruel seas like mountains fill the bay,
Wrecking the quayside huts,
Salting our vineyards with tall showers of spray;

And though the moon shines dangerously clear,
Fixed in another cycle
Than the sun's progress round the felloe'd year;

And though I may not hope to dwell apart
With you on Apple Island
Unless my breast be docile to the dart—

Why should I fear your element, the sea,
Or the full moon, your mirror,
Or the halved apple from your holy tree?

ROBERT GRAVES

All Except Hannibal

Trapped in a dismal marsh, he told his troops:
'No lying down, lads! Form your own mess-groups
And sit in circles, each man on the knees
Of the man behind; then nobody will freeze.'

They obeyed his orders, as the cold sun set,
Drowsing all night in one another's debt,
All except Hannibal himself, who chose
His private tree-stump – he was one of those!

ROBERT GRAVES

Palm Tree King

Because I come from the West Indies
certain people in England seem to think
I is a expert on palm trees

So not wanting to sever dis link
with me native roots (know what ah mean?)
or to disappoint dese culture vulture
I does smile cool as seabreeze

and say to dem
which specimen
you interested in
cause you talking
to the right man
I is palm tree king
I know palm tree history
like de palm o me hand
In fact me navel string
bury under a palm tree

If you think de queen could wave
you ain't see nothing yet
till you see the Roystonea Regia
– that is the royal palm –
with she crown of leaves
waving calm-calm
over the blue Caribbean carpet
nearly 100 feet of royal highness

But let we get down to business
Tell me what you want to know
How tall a palm tree does grow?
What is the biggest coconut I ever see?
What is the average length of the leaf?

Don't expect me to be brief
cause palm tree history
is a long-long story
Anyway why you so interested
in length and circumference?
That kind of talk so ordinary
That don't touch the essence
of palm tree mystery
That is no challenge
to a palm tree historian like me

If you insist on statistics
why you don't pose a question
with some mathematical profundity?

Ask me something more tricky
like if a American tourist with a camera
take 9 minutes to climb a coconut tree
how long a English tourist without a camera
would take to climb the same coconut tree?

That is problem pardner
Now ah coming harder

If 6 straw hat
and half a dozen bikini
multiply by the same number of coconut tree
equal one postcard
how many square miles of straw hat
you need to make a tourist industry?

That is problem pardner
Find the solution
and you got a revolution

But before you say anything
let I palm tree king
give you dis warning
Ah want de answer in metric

it kind of rhyme with tropic
Besides it sound more exotic

Emergency Kit

When I find myself among a laughing tribe,
I know they hide something from me;
I conjure up a laughter box whose button I press
to outlaugh them all. As long as they hear their music,
they leave me free; I don't want to surrender all I have.
I am a moving stump in the forest of men
and if I stray into a towering company, those
more than a kilometre from the undergrowth,
I release stilts from my soles; I don't want to be
looked down upon by the very top ones.
I collapse the long legs when I step into where
giants are the required offerings to the gods of the race.
I have a lifesaver installed in my body
just in case I am knocked into some deep river;
unless I come out alive, I will be declared evil —
who ever wants his adversary to have the last word on him?
So when a hunter stalks me to fill his bag,
I call on my snake from nowhere to bite him.
Folks, let's drink ourselves to death in the party
as long as we wear sponges in the tongue;
let's stay awake in our unending dream so that nobody
will take us for gone and cheat us out of our lives.

The Transposition of Clermont

After the Big Flood, we elected
to move our small timber city
from the dangerous beauty of the river
and its fringed lagoons
since both had risen to destroy us.

Many buildings went stacked on wagons
but more were towed entire
in strained stateliness, with a long groyning sound,
up timber by traction engines.

Each moved singly. Life went on round them;
in them, at points of rest.
Guests at breakfast in the Royal Hotel, facing
now the saddlery, now the Town Hall.

We drank in the canted Freemasons
and the progressive Shamrock, but really
all pubs were the Exchange. Relativities
interchanged our world like a chess game:

butcher occluded baker, the police
eclipsed both brothels, the dance hall
sashayed around the Temperance Hall,
front doors sniffed rear, and thoughtfully ground on.

Certain houses burst, and vanished.
One wept its windows, one trailed mementoes up the street.
A taut chain suddenly parted and scythed down
horses and a verandah. Weed-edged black rectangles
in exploded gardens yielded sovereigns and spoons.

That ascent of working architecture
onto the pegged plateau was a children's crusade
with lines stretching down to us.
Everything standing in its wrong accustomed place.
My generation's memories are intricately transposed:

butcher occluding dance music, the police
eclipsed by opportunity, brothels sashaying royally
and, riding sidesaddle up shined skids, the Town Hall.
Excited, we would meet on streets that stayed immutable

sometimes for weeks; from irrecoverable corners
and alleys already widening, we'd look
back down at our new graves and childhood gardens,
the odd house at anchor for a quick tomato season
and the swaying nailed hull of a church going on before us.

And many allotments left unbought, or for expansion
never filled up, above, as they hadn't below.
What was town, what was country stayed elusive
as we saw it always does, in the bush,
what is waste, what is space, what is land.

LES MURRAY

Mercian Hymns

IX

The strange church smelled a bit 'high', of censers and polish.
    The strange curate was just as appropriate: he took off into
    the marriage-service. No one cared to challenge that gambit.

Then he dismissed you, and the rest of us followed, sheepish
    next-of-kin, to the place without the walls: spoil-heaps of
    chrysanths dead in their plastic macs, eldorado of wash-
    stand-marble.

Embarrassed, we dismissed ourselves: the three mute great-
    aunts borne away down St Chad's Garth in a stiff-backed
    Edwardian Rolls.

I unburden the saga of your burial, my dear. You had lived long
    enough to see things 'nicely settled'.

XII

Their spades grafted through the variably-resistant soil. They
  clove to the hoard. They ransacked epiphanies, vertebrae of
  the chimera, armour of wild bees' larvae. They struck the
  fire-dragon's faceted skin.

The men were paid to caulk water-pipes. They brewed and pissed
  amid splendour; their latrine seethed its estuary through
  nettles. They are scattered to your collations, moldywarp.

It is autumn. Chestnut-boughs clash their inflamed leaves. The
  garden festers for attention: telluric cultures enriched with
  shards, corms, nodules, the sunk solids of gravity. I have
  raked up a golden and stinking blaze.

GEOFFREY HILL

The Making of the Drum

1 *The Skin*

First the goat
must be killed
and the skin
stretched.

Bless you, four-footed animal, who eats rope,
skilled
upon rocks, horned with our sin;
stretch your skin, stretch

it tight on our hope;
we have killed
you to make a thin
voice that will reach

further than hope
further than heaven, that will

reach deep down to our gods where the thin
light cannot leak, where our stretched

hearts cannot leap. Cut the rope
of its throat, skilled
destroyer of goats; its sin,
spilled on the washed gravel, reaches

and spreads to devour us all. So the goat
must be killed
and its skin
stretched.

2 *The Barrel of the Drum*

For this we choose wood
of the *tweneduru* tree:
hard *duru* wood
with the hollow blood
that makes a womb.

Here in this silence
we hear the wounds
of the forest;
we hear the sounds
of the rivers;

vowels of reed-
lips, pebbles
of consonants,
underground dark
of the continent.

You dumb *adom* wood
will be bent,
will be solemnly bent, belly
rounded with fire, wound-
ed with tools

that will shape you.
You will bleed,
cedar dark,
when we cut you;
speak, when we touch you.

3 *The Two Curved Sticks of the Drummer*

There is a quick
stick grows in the for-
est, blossoms twice year-
ly without leaves;
bare white branches
crack like light-
ning in the harm-
attan.

But no harm
comes to those who live near-
by. This tree, the
elders say, will never
die.

From this stripped tree
snap quick sticks for
the festival. Its wood,
heat-hard as stone,
is toneless as a bone.

4 *Gourds and Rattles*

Cal-
abash trees'
leaves

do not clash;
bear a green
gourd, burn

copper in the
light, crack
open seeds
that rattle.

Blind underground the rat's
dark saw-teeth bleed
the wet root, snap
its slow long drag of time,

its grit, its flavour; turn
the ripe leaves sour. Clash
rattle, sing gourd; never leave
time's dancers weary like this tree
that makes and mocks our music.

5 *The Gong-Gong*

God is dumb
until the drum
speaks.

The drum
is dumb
until the gong-gong leads

it. Man made,
the gong-gong's
iron eyes

of music
walk us through the humble
dead to meet

the dumb
blind drum
where Odomankoma speaks:

EDWARD KAMAU BRATHWAITE

The Silent Piano

We have lived like civilized people.
O ruins, traditions!

And we have seen the barbarians,
breakers of sculpture and glass.

And now we talk of 'the inner life',
and I ask myself, where is it?

Not here, in these streets and houses,
so I think it must be found

in indolence, pure indolence,
an ocean of darkness,

in silence, an arm of the moon,
a hand that enters slowly.

*

I am reminded of a story
Camus tells, of a man in prison camp.

He had carved a piano keyboard
with a nail on a piece of wood.

And sat there playing the piano.
This music was made entirely of silence.

LOUIS SIMPSON

Bedtime Story

Long long ago when the world was a wild place
Planted with bushes and peopled by apes, our
Mission Brigade was at work in the jungle.
    Hard by the Congo

Once, when a foraging detail was active
Scouting for green-fly, it came on a grey man, the
Last living man, in the branch of a baobab
        Stalking a monkey.

Earlier men had disposed of, for pleasure,
Creatures whose names we scarcely remember –
Zebra, rhinoceros, elephants, wart-hog,
        Lion, rats, deer. But

After the wars had extinguished the cities
Only the wild ones were left, half-naked
Near the Equator: and here was the last one,
        Starved for a monkey.

By then the Mission Brigade had encountered
Hundreds of such men: and their procedure,
History tells us, was only to feed them:
        Find them and feed them;

Those were the orders. And this was the last one.
Nobody knew that he was, but he was. Mud
Caked on his flat grey flanks. He was crouched, half-
        armed with a shaved spear

Glinting beneath broad leaves. When their jaws cut
Swathes through the bark and he saw fine teeth shine,
Round eyes roll round and forked arms waver
        Huge as the rough trunks

Over his head, he was frightened. Our workers
Marched through the Congo before he was born, but
This was the first time perhaps that he'd seen one.
        Staring in hot still

Silence, he crouched there: then jumped. With a long swing
Down from his branch, he had angled his spear too
Quickly, before they could hold him, and hurled it
        Hard at the soldier

Leading the detail. How could he know Queen's
Orders were only to help him? The soldier
Winced when the tipped spear pricked him. Unsheathing his
    Sting was a reflex.

Later the Queen was informed. There were no more
Men. An impetuous soldier had killed off,
Purely by chance, the penultimate primate.
    When she was certain,

Squadrons of workers were fanned through the Congo
Detailed to bring back the man's picked bones to be
Sealed in the archives in amber. I'm quite sure
    Nobody found them

After the most industrious search, though.
Where had the bones gone? Over the earth, dear,
Ground by the teeth of the termites, blown by the
    Wind, like the dodo's.

GEORGE MACBETH

The Horses

Barely a twelvemonth after
The seven days war that put the world to sleep,
Late in the evening the strange horses came.
By then we had made our covenant with silence,
But in the first few days it was so still
We listened to our breathing and were afraid.
On the second day
The radios failed; we turned the knobs; no answer.
On the third day a warship passed us, heading north,
Dead bodies piled on the deck. On the sixth day
A plane plunged over us into the sea. Thereafter
Nothing. The radios dumb;
And still they stand in corners of our kitchens,

And stand, perhaps, turned on, in a million rooms
All over the world. But now if they should speak,
If on a sudden they should speak again,
If on the stroke of noon a voice should speak,
We would not listen, we would not let it bring
That old bad world that swallowed its children quick
At one great gulp. We would not have it again.
Sometimes we think of the nations lying asleep,
Curled blindly in impenetrable sorrow,
And then the thought confounds us with its strangeness.
The tractors lie about our fields; at evening
They look like dank sea-monsters couched and waiting.
We leave them where they are and let them rust:
'They'll moulder away and be like other loam.'
We make our oxen drag our rusty ploughs,
Long laid aside. We have gone back
Far past our fathers' land.

                              And then, that evening
Late in the summer the strange horses came.
We heard a distant tapping on the road,
A deepening drumming; it stopped, went on again
And at the corner changed to hollow thunder.
We saw the heads
Like a wild wave charging and were afraid.
We had sold our horses in our fathers' time
To buy new tractors. Now they were strange to us
As fabulous steeds set on an ancient shield
Or illustrations in a book of knights.
We did not dare go near them. Yet they waited,
Stubborn and shy, as if they had been sent
By an old command to find our whereabouts
And that long-lost archaic companionship.
In the first moment we had never a thought
That they were creatures to be owned and used.
Among them were some half-a-dozen colts
Dropped in some wilderness of the broken world,

Yet new as if they had come from their own Eden.
Since then they have pulled our ploughs and borne our loads
But that free servitude still can pierce our hearts.
Our life is changed; their coming our beginning.

EDWIN MUIR

Johann Joachim Quantz's Five Lessons

The First Lesson

So that each person may quickly find that
Which particularly concerns him, certain metaphors
Convenient to us within the compass of this
Lesson are to be allowed. It is best I sit
Here where I am to speak on the other side
Of language. You, of course, in your own time
And incident (I speak in the small hours.)
Will listen from your side. I am very pleased
We have sought us out. No doubt you have read
My Flute Book. Come. The Guild clock's iron men
Are striking out their few deserted hours
And here from my high window Brueghel's winter
Locks the canal below. I blow my fingers.

The Second Lesson

Good morning, Karl. Sit down. I have been thinking
About your progress and my progress as one
Who teaches you, a young man with talent
And the rarer gift of application. I think
You must now be becoming a musician
Of a certain calibre. It is right maybe
That in our lessons now I should expect
Slight and very polite impatiences
To show in you. Karl, I think it is true,
You are now nearly able to play the flute.

Now we must try higher, aware of the terrible
Shapes of silence sitting outside your ear
Anxious to define you and really love you.
Remember silence is curious about its opposite
Element which you shall learn to represent.

Enough of that. Now stand in the correct position
So that the wood of the floor will come up through you.
Stand, but not too stiff. Keep your elbows down.
Now take a simple breath and make me a shape
Of clear unchained started and finished tones.
Karl, as well as you are able, stop
Your fingers into the breathing apertures
And speak and make the cylinder delight us.

The Third Lesson

Karl, you are late. The traverse flute is not
A study to take lightly. I am cold waiting.
Put one piece of coal in the stove. This lesson
Shall not be prolonged. Right. Stand in your place.

Ready? Blow me a little ladder of sound
From a good stance so that you feel the heavy
Press of the floor coming up through you and
Keeping your pitch and tone in character.

Now that is something, Karl. You are getting on.
Unswell your head. One more piece of coal.
Go on now but remember it must be always
Easy and flowing. Light and shadow must
Be varied but be varied in your mind
Before you hear the eventual return sound.

Play me the dance you made for the barge-master.
Stop stop Karl. Play it as you first thought
Of it in the hot boat-kitchen. That is a pleasure
For me. I can see I am making you good.
Keep the stove red. Hand me the matches. Now

We can see better. Give me a shot at the pipe.
Karl, I can still put on a good flute-mouth
And show you in this high cold room something
You will be famous to have said you heard.

The Fourth Lesson

You are early this morning. What we have to do
Today is think of you as a little creator
After the big creator. And it can be argued
You are as necessary, even a composer
Composing in the flesh an attitude
To slay the ears of the gentry. Karl,
I know you find great joy in the great
Composers. But now you can put your lips to
The messages and blow them into sound
And enter and be there as well. You must
Be faithful to who you are speaking from
And yet it is all right. You will be there.

Take your coat off. Sit down. A glass of Bols
Will help us both. I think you are good enough
To not need me anymore. I think you know
You are not only an interpreter.
What you will do is always something else
And they will hear you simultaneously with
The Art you have been given to read. Karl,

I think the Spring is really coming at last.
I see the canal boys working. I realize
I have not asked you to play the flute today.
Come and look. Are the barges not moving?
You must forgive me. I am not myself today.
Be here on Thursday. When you come, bring
Me five herrings. Watch your fingers. Spring
Is apparent but it is still chilblain weather.

The Last Lesson

Dear Karl, this morning is our last lesson.
I have been given the opportunity to
Live in a certain person's house and tutor
Him and his daughters on the traverse flute.
Karl, you will be all right. In those recent
Lessons my heart lifted to your playing.

I know. I see you doing well, invited
In a great chamber in front of the gentry. I
Can see them with their dresses settling in
And bored mouths beneath moustaches sizing
You up as you are, a lout from the canal
With big ears but an angel's tread on the flute.

But you will be all right. Stand in your place
Before them. Remember Johann. Begin with good
Nerve and decision. Do not intrude too much
Into the message you carry and put out.

One last thing, Karl, remember when you enter
The joy of those quick high archipelagoes,
To make to keep your finger-stops as light
As feathers but definite. What can I say more?
Do not be sentimental or in your Art.
I will miss you. Do not expect applause.

W. S. GRAHAM

Variations for Two Pianos

for Thomas Higgins, pianist

There is no music now in all Arkansas.
Higgins is gone, taking both his pianos.

Movers dismantled the instruments, away
Sped the vans. The first detour untuned the strings.
There is no music now in all Arkansas.

Up Main Street, past the cold shopfronts of Conway,
The brash, self-important brick of the college,
Higgins is gone, taking both his pianos.

Warm evenings, the windows open, he would play
Something of Mozart's for his pupils, the birds.
There is no music now in all Arkansas.

How shall the mockingbird mend her trill, the jay
His eccentric attack, lacking a teacher?
Higgins is gone, taking both his pianos.

There is no music now in all Arkansas.

DONALD JUSTICE

An American Roadside Elegy

Already the creamy Volkswagen rocks back
into the dust, its smooth dome
split like a man's head,
gouged by gravel, one or two
Budweiser cans squashed
among whiskers of chickweed.
They are watching, who yet own
the night's little pockets
of darkness where moonlight crawls.
We remember our brother who died
mouth open in this red dirt.
Murdered, we say. It's Spring,
a green urge on the sides
of concrete walls at the Dew-Drop Inn.
They were here, Joe and the girl,

white, glued to his brown rib,
until the pond of the hill
lay silver as a bedsheet
wrinkled, and their wanting done.
There's not much to go on. The sound
of glass speaking, a raw instant
the chassis rocked up to hang
free a hand in the window,
as if she chose to sleep.
What did the stones say
they couldn't answer ever?
The morning comes cool, sweet.
James Brown touts a new bag
on the radio. Daffodils luff.
In the country store we stop years
later, getting out at the scene,
flashers on, gravel hissing
as always. Cows watch.
Fists of Southern boys pose
on fenders, sweaty, as if they
know they wait in the truth.
As if they expected to be him,
but it wasn't their time
to go face up, to grin
into the sun and the moon
so steadily. As he liked to do.

DAVE SMITH

The Dream of Wearing Shorts Forever

To go home and wear shorts forever
in the enormous paddocks, in that warm climate,
adding a sweater when winter soaks the grass,

to camp out along the river bends
for good, wearing shorts, with a pocketknife,
a fishing line and matches,

or there where the hills are all down, below the plain,
to sit around in shorts at evening
on the plank verandah —

If the cardinal points of costume
are Robes, Tato, Rig and Scunge,
where are shorts in this compass?

They are never Robes
as other bareleg outfits have been:
the toga, the kilt, the lava-lava,
the Mahatma's cotton dhoti;

archbishops and field marshals
at their ceremonies never wear shorts.
The very word
means underpants in North America.

Shorts can be Tat,
Land-Rovering, bush-environmental tat,
socio-political ripped-and-metal-stapled tat,
solidarity-with-the-Third World tat tvam asi,

likewise track-and-field shorts worn to parties
and the further humid, modelling negligée
of the Kingdom of Flaunt,
that unchallenged aristocracy.

More plainly climatic, shorts
are farmers' rig, leathery with salt and bonemeal,
are sailors' and branch bankers' rig,
the crisp golfing style
of our youngest male National Costume.

Most loosely, they are Scunge,
ancient Bengal bloomers or moth-eaten hot pants

worn with a former shirt,
feet, beach sand, hair
and a paucity of signals.

Scunge, which is real negligée,
housework in a swimsuit, pyjamas worn all day,
is holiday, is freedom from ambition.
Scunge makes you invisible
to the world and yourself.

The entropy of costume,
scunge can get you conquered by more vigorous cultures
and help you to notice it less.

To be or to become
is a serious question posed by a work-shorts counter
with its pressed stacks, bulk khaki and blue,
reading Yakka or King Gee, crisp with steely warehouse odour.

Satisfied ambition, defeat, true unconcern,
the wish and the knack for self-forgetfulness
all fall within the scunge ambit
wearing board shorts or similar;
it is a kind of weightlessness.

Unlike public nakedness, which in Westerners
is deeply circumstantial, relaxed as exam time,
artless and equal as the corsetry of a hussar regiment,

shorts and their plain like
are an angelic nudity,
spirituality with pockets!
A double updraft as you drop from branch to pool!

Ideal for getting served last
in shops of the temperate zone
they are also ideal for going home, into space,
into time, to farm the mind's Sabine acres
for product or subsistence.

– Now that everyone who yearned to wear long pants
has essentially achieved them,
long pants, which have themselves been underwear
repeatedly, and underground more than once,
it is time perhaps to cherish the culture of shorts,

to moderate grim vigour
with the knobble of bare knees,
to cool bareknuckle feet in inland water,
slapping flies with a book on solar wind
or a patient bare hand, beneath the cadjiput trees,

to be walking meditatively
among green timber, through the grassy forest
towards a calm sea
and looking across to more of that great island
and the further tropics.

LES MURRAY

Swineherd

When all this is over, said the swineherd,
I mean to retire, where
Nobody will have heard about my special skills
And conversation is mainly about the weather.

I intend to learn how to make coffee, at least as well
As the Portuguese lay-sister in the kitchen
And polish the brass fenders every day.
I want to lie awake at night
Listening to cream crawling to the top of the jug
And the water lying soft in the cistern.

I want to see an orchard where the trees grow in straight lines
And the yellow fox finds shelter between the navy-blue trunks,

Where it gets dark early in summer
And the apple-blossom is allowed to wither on the bough.

EILÉAN NÍ CHUILLEANÁIN

Studying the Language

On Sundays I watch the hermits coming out of their holes
Into the light. Their cliff is as full as a hive.
They crowd together on warm shoulders of rock
Where the sun has been shining, their joints crackle.
They begin to talk after a while.
I listen to their accents, they are not all
From this island, not all old,
Not even, I think, all masculine.

They are so wise, they do not pretend to see me.
They drink from the scattered pools of melted snow:
I walk right by them and drink when they have done.
I can see the marks of chains around their feet.

I call this my work, these decades and stations –
Because, without these, I would be a stranger here.

EILÉAN NÍ CHUILLEANÁIN

Diving into the Wreck

First having read the book of myths,
and loaded the camera,
and checked the edge of the knife-blade,
I put on
the body-armor of black rubber
the absurd flippers
the grave and awkward mask.
I am having to do this

not like Cousteau with his
assiduous team
aboard the sun-flooded schooner
but here alone.

There is a ladder.
The ladder is always there
hanging innocently
close to the side of the schooner.
We know what it is for,
we who have used it.
Otherwise
it's a piece of maritime floss
some sundry equipment.

I go down.
Rung after rung and still
the oxygen immerses me
the blue light
the clear atoms
of our human air.
I go down.
My flippers cripple me,
I crawl like an insect down the ladder
and there is no one
to tell me when the ocean
will begin.

First the air is blue and then
it is bluer and then green and then
black I am blacking out and yet
my mask is powerful
it pumps my blood with power
the sea is another story
the sea is not a question of power
I have to learn alone
to turn my body without force
in the deep element.

And now: it is easy to forget
what I came for
among so many who have always
lived here
swaying their crenellated fans
between the reefs
and besides
you breathe differently down here.

I came to explore the wreck.
The words are purposes.
The words are maps.
I came to see the damage that was done
and the treasures that prevail.
I stroke the beam of my lamp
slowly along the flank
of something more permanent
than fish or weed

the thing I came for:
the wreck and not the story of the wreck
the thing itself and not the myth
the drowned face always staring
toward the sun
the evidence of damage
worn by salt and sway into this threadbare beauty
the ribs of the disaster
curving their assertion
among the tentative haunters.

This is the place.
And I am here, the mermaid whose dark hair
streams black, the merman in his armored body
We circle silently
about the wreck
we dive into the hold.
I am she: I am he

whose drowned face sleeps with open eyes
whose breasts still bear the stress
whose silver, copper, vermeil cargo lies
obscurely inside barrels
half-wedged and left to rot
we are the half-destroyed instruments
that once held to a course
the water-eaten log
the fouled compass

We are, I am, you are
by cowardice or courage
the one who find our way
back to this scene
carrying a knife, a camera
a book of myths
in which
our names do not appear.

ADRIENNE RICH

Punishment

I can feel the tug
of the halter at the nape
of her neck, the wind
on her naked front.

It blows her nipples
to amber beads,
it shakes the frail rigging
of her ribs.

I can see her drowned
body in the bog,
the weighing stone,
the floating rods and boughs.

Under which at first
she was a barked sapling
that is dug up
oak-bone, brain-firkin:

her shaved head
like a stubble of black corn,
her blindfold a soiled bandage,
her noose a ring

to store
the memories of love.
Little adulteress,
before they punished you

you were flaxen-haired,
undernourished, and your
tar-black face was beautiful.
My poor scapegoat,

I almost love you
but would have cast, I know,
the stones of silence.
I am the artful voyeur

of your brain's exposed
and darkened combs,
your muscles' webbing
and all your numbered bones:

I who have stood dumb
when your betraying sisters,
cauled in tar,
wept by the railings,

who would connive
in civilized outrage
yet understand the exact
and tribal, intimate revenge.

SEAMUS HEANEY

[55]

A Disused Shed in County Wexford

for J. G. Farrell

Let them not forget us, the weak souls among the asphodels
SEFERIS, 'Mythistorema'

Even now there are places where a thought might grow —
Peruvian mines, worked out and abandoned
To a slow clock of condensation,
An echo trapped for ever, and a flutter of
Wild flowers in the lift-shaft,
Indian compounds where the wind dances
And a door bangs with diminished confidence.
Lime crevices behind rippling rain-barrels,
Dog-corners for shit-burials;
And in a disused shed in County Wexford,

Deep in the grounds of a burnt-out hotel,
Among the bath-tubs and the wash-basins
A thousand mushrooms crowd to a keyhole.
This is the one star in their firmament
Or frames a star within a star.
What should they do there but desire?
So many days beyond the rhododendrons
With the world waltzing in its bowl of cloud,
They have learnt patience and silence
Listening to the rooks querulous in the high wood.

They have been waiting for us in a foetor of
Vegetable sweat since civil-war days,
Since the gravel-crunching, interminable departure
Of the expropriated mycologist.
He never came back, and light since then
Is a keyhole rusting gently after rain.
Spiders have spun, flies dusted to mildew
And once a day, perhaps, they have heard something —
A trickle of masonry, a shout from the blue
Or a lorry changing gear at the end of the lane.

There have been deaths, the pale flesh flaking
Into the earth that nourished it;
And nightmares, born of these and the grim
Dominion of stale air and rank moisture.
Those nearest the door grow strong –
Elbow room! – Elbow room!
The rest, dim in a twilight of crumbling
Utensils and broken pitchers, groaning
For their deliverance, have been so long
Expectant that there is left only the posture.

A half-century, without visitors, in the dark –
Poor preparation for the cracking lock
And creak of hinges. Magi, moon-men,
Powdery prisoners of the old regime,
Web-throated, stalked like triffids, racked by drouth
And insomnia, only the ghost of a scream
At the flash-bulb firing-squad we wake them with
Shows there is life yet in their feverish forms.
Grown beyond nature now, soft food for worms,
They lift frail heads in gravity and good faith.

They are begging us, you see, in their wordless way,
To do something, to speak on their behalf
Or at least not to close the door again.
Lost people of Treblinka and Pompeii!
Save us, save us, they seem to say;
Let the god not abandon us
Who have come so far in darkness and in pain.
We too had our lives to live.
You with your light meter and relaxed itinerary,
Let not our naive labours have been in vain.

DEREK MAHON

The Bright Lights of Sarajevo

After the hours that Sarajevans pass
queuing with empty canisters of gas
to get the refills they wheel home in prams,
or queuing for the precious meagre grams
of bread they're rationed to each day,
and often dodging snipers on the way,
or struggling up sometimes eleven flights
of stairs with water, then you'd think the nights
of Sarajevo would be totally devoid
of people walking streets Serb shells destroyed,
but tonight in Sarajevo that's just not the case—
the young go walking at a stroller's pace,
black shapes impossible to mark
as Muslim, Serb or Croat in such dark,
in unlit streets you can't distinguish who
calls bread *hjleb* or *hleb* or calls it *kruh*.
All take the evening air with stroller's stride,
no torches guide them, but they don't collide
except as one of the flirtatious ploys
when a girl's dark shape is fancied by a boy's.
Then the tender radar of the tone of voice
shows by its signals she approves his choice.
Then match or lighter to a cigarette
to check in her eyes if he's made progress yet.

And I see a pair who've certainly progressed
beyond the tone of voice and match-flare test
and he's about, I think, to take her hand
and lead her away from where they stand
on two shell scars, where, in 1992
Serb mortars massacred the breadshop queue
and blood-dunked crusts of shredded bread
lay on this pavement with the broken dead.
And at their feet in holes made by the mortar

that caused the massacre, now full of water
from the rain that's poured down half the day,
though now even the smallest clouds have cleared away,
leaving the Sarajevo star-filled evening sky
ideally bright and clear for bomber's eye,
in those two rain-full shell-holes the boy sees
fragments of the splintered Pleiades,
sprinkled on those death-deep, death-dark wells
splashed on the pavement by Serb mortar shells.

The dark boy-shape leads dark girl-shape away
to share one coffee in a candlelit café
until the curfew, and he holds her hand
behind AID flour-sacks refilled with sand.

TONY HARRISON

Lightenings: viii

The annals say: when the monks of Clonmacnoise
Were all at prayers inside the oratory
A ship appeared above them in the air.

The anchor dragged along behind so deep
It hooked itself into the altar rails
And then, as the big hull rocked to a standstill,

A crewman shinned and grappled down the rope
And struggled to release it. But in vain.
'This man can't bear our life here and will drown,'

The abbot said, 'unless we help him.' So
They did, the freed ship sailed, and the man climbed back
Out of the marvellous as he had known it.

SEAMUS HEANEY

The Season of Phantasmal Peace

Then all the nations of birds lifted together
the huge net of the shadows of this earth
in multitudinous dialects, twittering tongues,
stitching and crossing it. They lifted up
the shadows of long pines down trackless slopes,
the shadows of glass-faced towers down evening streets,
the shadow of a frail plant on a city sill—
the net rising soundless as night, the birds' cries soundless,
     until
there was no longer dusk, or season, decline, or weather,
only this passage of phantasmal light
that not the narrowest shadow dared to sever.

And men could not see, looking up, what the wild geese drew,
what the ospreys trailed behind them in silvery ropes
that flashed in the icy sunlight; they could not hear
battalions of starlings waging peaceful cries,
bearing the net higher, covering this world
like the vines of an orchard, or a mother drawing
the trembling gauze over the trembling eyes
of a child fluttering to sleep;
                                   it was the light
that you will see at evening on the side of a hill
in yellow October, and no one hearing knew
what change had brought into the raven's cawing,
the killdeer's screech, the ember-circling chough
such an immense, soundless, and high concern
for the fields and cities where the birds belong,
except it was their seasonal passing, Love,
made seasonless, or, from the high privilege of their birth,
something brighter than pity for the wingless ones
below them who shared dark holes in windows and in houses,
and higher they lifted the net with soundless voices
above all change, betrayals of falling suns,

and this season lasted one moment, like the pause
between dusk and darkness, between fury and peace,
but, for such as our earth is now, it lasted long.

DEREK WALCOTT

From the Domain of Arnheim

And so that all these ages, these years
we cast behind us, like the smoke-clouds
dragged back into vacancy when the rocket springs—

The domain of Arnheim was all snow, but we were there.
We saw a yellow light thrown on the icefield
from the huts by the pines, and laughter came up
floating from a white corrie
miles away, clearly.
We moved on down, arm in arm.
I know you would have thought it was a dream
but we were there. And those were trumpets—
tremendous round the rocks—
while they were burning fires of trash and mammoths' bones.
They sang naked, and kissed in the smoke.
A child, or one of their animals, was crying.
Young men blew the ice crystals off their drums.
We came down among them, but of course
they could see nothing, on their time-scale.
Yet they sensed us, stopped, looked up – even into our eyes.
To them we were a displacement of the air,
a sudden chill, yet we had no power
over their fear. If one of them had been dying
he would have died. The crying
came from one just born: that was the cause
of the song. We saw it now. What had we stopped
but joy?
I know you felt

the same dismay, you gripped my arm, they were waiting
for what they knew of us to pass.
A sweating trumpeter took
a brand from the fire with a shout and threw it
where our bodies would have been –
we felt nothing but his courage.
And so they would deal with every imagined power
seen or unseen.
There are no gods in the domain of Arnheim.

We signalled to the ship; got back;
our lives and days returned to us, but
haunted by deeper souvenirs than any rocks or seeds.
From time the souvenirs are deeds.

EDWIN MORGAN

Ghetto

I

Because you will suffer soon and die, your choices
Are neither right nor wrong: a spoon will feed you,
A flannel keep you clean, a toothbrush bring you back
To your bathroom's view of chimney-pots and gardens.
With so little time for inventory or leavetaking,
You are packing now for the rest of your life
Photographs, medicines, a change of underwear, a book,
A candlestick, a loaf, sardines, needle and thread.
These are your heirlooms, perishables, worldly goods.
What you bring is the same as what you leave behind,
Your last belonging a list of your belongings.

II

As though it were against the law to sleep on pillows
They have filled a cathedral with confiscated feathers:
Silence irrefrangible, no room for angels' wings,
Tons of feathers suffocating cherubim and seraphim.

III

The little girl without a mother behaves like a mother
With her rag doll to whom she explains fear and anguish,
The meagreness of the bread ration, how to make it last,
How to get back to the doll's house and lift up the roof
And, before the flame-throwers and dynamiters destroy it,
How to rescue from their separate rooms love and sorrow,
Masterpieces the size of a postage stamp, small fortunes.

IV

From among the hundreds of thousands I can imagine one
Behind the barbed-wire fences as my train crosses Poland.
I see him for long enough to catch the sprinkle of snowflakes
On his hair and schoolbag, and then I am transported
Away from that world of broken hobby-horses and silent toys.
He turns into a little snowman and refuses to melt.

V

For street-singers in the marketplace, weavers, warp-makers,
Those who suffer in sewing-machine repair shops, excrement-
Removal workers, there are not enough root vegetables,
Beetroots, turnips, swedes, nor for the leather-stitchers
Who are boiling leather so that their children may eat;
Who are turning like a thick slice of potato-bread
This page, which is everything I know about potatoes,
My delivery of Irish Peace, Beauty of Hebron, Home
Guard, Arran Banners, Kerr's Pinks, resistant to eelworm,
Resignation, common scab, terror, frost, potato-blight.

VI

There will be performances in the waiting room, and time
To jump over a skipping rope, and time to adjust
As though for a dancing class the ribbons in your hair.
This string quartet is the most natural thing in the world.

VII

Fingers leave shadows on a violin, harmonics,
A blackbird fluttering between electrified fences.

VIII

Lessons were forbidden in that terrible school.
Punishable by death were reading and writing
And arithmetic, so that even the junior infants
Grew old and wise in lofts studying these subjects.
There were drawing lessons, and drawings of kitchens
And farms, farm animals, butterflies, mothers, fathers
Who survived in crayon until in pen and ink
They turned into guards at executions and funerals
Torturing and hanging even these stick figures.
There were drawings of barracks and latrines as well
And the only windows were the windows they drew.

MICHAEL LONGLEY

Before

Make over the alleys and gardens to birdsong,
The hour of not-for-an-hour. Lie still.
Leave the socks you forgot on the clothesline.
Leave slugs to make free with the pansies.
The jets will give Gatwick a miss
And from here you could feel the springs
Wake by the doorstep and under the precinct

Where now there is nobody frozenly waiting.
This is free time, in the sense that a handbill
Goes cartwheeling over the crossroads
Past stoplights rehearsing in private
And has neither witness nor outcome.
This is before the first bus has been late
Or the knickers sought under the bed
Or the first cigarette undertaken,
Before the first flush and cross word.
Viaducts, tunnels and motorways: still.
The mines and the Japanese sunrise: still.
The high bridges lean out in the wind
On the curve of their pinkening lights,
And the coast is inert as a model.
The wavebands are empty, the mail unimagined
And bacon still wrapped in the freezer
Like evidence aimed to intrigue our successors.
The island is dreamless, its slack-jawed insomniacs
Stunned by the final long shot of the movie,
Its murderers innocent, elsewhere.
The policemen have slipped from their helmets
And money forgets how to count.
In the bowels of Wapping the telephones
Shamelessly rest in their cradles.
The bomb in the conference centre's
A harmless confection of elements
Strapped to a duct like an art installation.
The Première sleeps in her fashion,
Her Majesty, all the princesses, tucked up
With the Bishops, the glueys, the DHSS,
In the People's Republic of Zeds.
And you sleep at my shoulder, the cat at your feet,
And deserve to be spared the irruption
Of if, but and ought, which is why
I declare this an hour of general safety
When even the personal monster—

Example, the Kraken – is dead to the world
Like the deaf submarines with their crewmen
Spark out at their fathomless consoles.
No one has died. There need be no regret,
For we do not exist, and I promise
I shall not wake anyone yet.

SEAN O'BRIEN

Swimming in the Flood

Later he must have watched
the newsreel,

his village erased by water: farmsteads and churches
breaking and floating away

as if by design;
bloated cattle, lumber, bales of straw,

turning in local whirlpools; the camera
panning across the surface, finding the odd

rooftop or skeletal tree,
or homing in to focus on a child's

shock-headed doll.
Under it all, his house would be standing intact,

the roses and lime trees, the windows,
the baby grand.

He saw it through the water when he dreamed
and, waking at night, he remembered the rescue boat,

the chickens at the prow, his neighbour's pig,
the woman beside him, clutching a silver frame,

her face dislodged, reduced to a puzzle of bone
and atmosphere, the tremors on her skin

wayward and dark, like shadows crossing a field
of clouded grain.

Later, he would see her on the screen,
trying to smile, as they lifted her on to the dock,

and he'd notice the frame again, baroque and absurd,
and empty, like the faces of the drowned.

JOHN BURNSIDE

A Surprise in the Peninsula

When I came in that night I found
the skin of a dog stretched flat and
nailed upon my wall between the
two windows. It seemed freshly killed—
there was blood at the edges. Not
my dog: I have never owned one,
I rather dislike them. (Perhaps
whoever did it knew that.) It
was a light brown dog, with smooth hair;
no head, but the tail still remained.
On the flat surface of the pelt
was branded the outline of the
peninsula, singed in thick black
strokes into the fur: a coarse map.
The position of the town was
marked by a bullet-hole; it went
right through the wall. I placed my eye
to it, and could see the dark trees
outside the house, flecked with moonlight.
I locked the door then, and sat up
all night, drinking small cups of the
bitter local coffee. A dog
would have been useful, I thought, for

protection. But perhaps the one
I had been given performed that
function; for no one came that night,
nor for three more. On the fourth day
it was time to leave. The dog-skin
still hung on the wall, stiff and dry
by now, the flies and the smell gone.
Could it, I wondered, have been meant
not as a warning, but a gift?
And, scarcely shuddering, I drew
the nails out and took it with me.

FLEUR ADCOCK

The Visible Baby

A large transparent baby like a skeleton in a red tree,
Like a little skeleton in the rootlet-pattern;
He is not of glass, this baby, his flesh is see-through,
Otherwise he is quite the same as any other baby.

I can see the white caterpillar of his milk looping through him,
I can see the pearl-bubble of his wind and stroke it out of him,
I can see his little lungs breathing like pink parks of trees,
I can see his little brain in its glass case like a budding rose;

There are his teeth in his transparent gums like a budding
    hawthorn twig,
His eyes like open poppies follow the light,
His tongue is like a crest of his thumping blood,
His heart like two squirrels one scarlet, one purple
Mating in the canopy of a blood-tree;

His spine like a necklace, all silvery-strung with cartilages,
His handbones like a working-party of white insects,
His nerves like a tree of ice with sunlight shooting through it,

What a closed book bound in wrinkled illustrations his father
    is to him!

PETER REDGROVE

Child Burial

Your coffin looked unreal,
fancy as a wedding cake.

I chose your grave clothes with care,
your favourite stripey shirt,

your blue cotton trousers.
They smelt of woodsmoke, of October,

your own smell there too.
I chose a gansy of handspun wool,

warm and fleecy for you. It is
so cold down in the dark.

No light can reach you and teach you
the paths of wild birds,

the names of the flowers,
the fishes, the creatures.

Ignorant you must remain
of the sun and its work,

my lamb, my calf, my eaglet,
my cub, my kid, my nestling,

my suckling, my colt. I would spin
time back, take you again

within my womb, your amniotic lair,
and further spin you back

through nine waxing months
to the split seeding moment

you chose to be made flesh,
word within me.

I'd cancel the love feast
the hot night of your making.

I would travel alone
to a quiet mossy place,

you would spill from me into the earth
drop by bright red drop.

PAULA MEEHAN

Cut

for Susan O'Neill Roe

What a thrill—
My thumb instead of an onion.
The top quite gone
Except for a sort of a hinge

Of skin,
A flap like a hat,
Dead white.
Then that red plush.

Little pilgrim,
The Indian's axed your scalp.
Your turkey wattle
Carpet rolls

Straight from the heart.
I step on it,
Clutching my bottle
Of pink fizz.

A celebration, this is.
Out of a gap
A million soldiers run,
Redcoats, every one.

Whose side are they on?
O my
Homunculus, I am ill.
I have taken a pill to kill

The thin
Papery feeling.
Saboteur,
Kamikaze man—

The stain on your
Gauze Ku Klux Klan
Babushka
Darkens and tarnishes and when

The balled
Pulp of your heart
Confronts its small
Mill of silence

How you jump—
Trepanned veteran,
Dirty girl,
Thumb stump.

SYLVIA PLATH

Two Songs

I

Sex, as they harshly call it,
I fell into this morning
at ten o'clock, a drizzling hour

of traffic and wet newspapers.
I thought of him who yesterday
clearly didn't
turn me to a hot field
ready for plowing,
and longing for that young man
piercèd me to the roots
bathing every vein, etc.
All day he appears to me
touchingly desirable,
a prize one could wreck one's peace for.
I'd call it love if love
didn't take so many years
but lust too is a jewel
a sweet flower and what
pure happiness to know
all our high-toned questions
breed in a lively animal.

    2

That 'old last act'!
And yet sometimes
all seems post coitum triste
and I a mere bystander.
Somebody else is going off,
getting shot to the moon.
Or, a moon-race!
Split seconds after
my opposite number lands
I make it—
we lie fainting together
at a crater-edge
heavy as mercury in our moonsuits
till he speaks—
in a different language

yet one I've picked up
through cultural exchanges...
we murmur the first moonwords:
Spasibo. Thanks. OK.

ADRIENNE RICH

'O little one, this longing is the pits'

O little one, this longing is the pits.
I'm horny as a timber wolf in heat.
Three times a night, a tangle up the sheet.
I seem to flirt with everything with tits:
Karyn at lunch, who knows I think she's cute;
my ex, the D.A. on the Sex Crimes Squad;
Iva's gnarled, canny New England god-
mother, who was my Saturday night date.
I'm trying to take things one at a time:
situps at bedtime, less coffee, less meat,
more showers, till a remedy appears.
Since there's already quite enough Sex Crime,
I think I ought to be kept off the street.
What are you doing for the next five years?

MARILYN HACKER

Ecstasy

As we made love for the third day,
cloudy and dark, as we did not stop
but went into it and into it and
did not hesitate and did not hold back we
rose through the air, until we were up above
timber line. The lake lay
icy and silver, the surface shirred,

reflecting nothing. The black rocks
lifted around it into the grainy
sepia air, the patches of snow
brilliant white, and even though we
did not know where we were, we could not
speak the language, we could hardly see, we
did not stop, rising with the black
rocks to the black hills, the black
mountains rising from the hills. Resting
on the crest of the mountains, one huge
cloud with scalloped edges of blazing
evening light, we did not turn back,
we stayed with it, even though we were
far beyond what we knew, we rose
into the grain of the cloud, even though we were
frightened, the air hollow, even though
nothing grew there, even though it is a
place from which no one has ever come back.

SHARON OLDS

Coming

is the body's way
of weeping, after a series
of shocks is suffered, after the thrust
of things, the gist of things, becomes
apparent: the bolt is felt completely
swollen in vicinity to wrench,
the skid is clearly headed
toward an all-out insult, and the senses
one by one abandon all their stations—
into smaller hours and thinner
minutes, seconds
split – till POW–

you had it, had it coming, and it heaved, whose participle
wasn't heaven.
That
was that.
And when you got

some senses back,
you asked yourself, is this
a dignified being's way
of being born? What
a thought
somebody had! (or some no-body)

out of the breathless blue, making us
double up like this, half gifted and
half robbed. 'Rise up to me,' the spirit

laughed. 'I'm
coming, I'm coming,'
the body sobbed.

HEATHER MCHUGH

Spilt Milk

Two soluble aspirins spore in this glass, their mycelia
fruiting the water, which I twist into milkiness.
The whole world seems to slide into the drain by my window.

It has rained and rained since you left, the streets black
and muscled with water. Out of pain and exhaustion you came
into my mouth, covering my tongue with your good and bitter
    milk.

Now I find you have cashed that cheque. I imagine you
slipping the paper under steel and glass. I sit here in a circle
of lamplight, studying women of nine hundred years past.

My hand moves into darkness as I write 'The adulterous
      woman
lost her nose and ears; the man was fined.' I drain the glass.
I still want to return to that hotel room by the station

to hear all night the goods trains coming and leaving.

SARAH MAGUIRE

Maura

She had never desired him in that way –
that aching in the skin she'd sometimes get
for a man possessed of that animal something.

Something outside of language or regret. No,
he'd been the regular husband, the hedged bet
against the baglady and spinsterhood;

a cap on the toothpaste, the mowed lawn, bills paid;
a well-insured warm body in the bed,
the kindly touch if seldom kindling.

Odd then, to have a grief so passionate
it woke her damp from dreams astraddle him –
the phantom embraced in pillows and blankets,

or sniffed among old shirts and bureau drawers.
She fairly swooned sometimes remembering
the curl of her name in his dull tenor.

Sweet nothings now rewhispered in her ears.
She chose black lace, black satin, reckoning
such pain a kind of romance in reverse.

The house filled with flowers. She ate nothing.
Giddy and sleepless, she longed for him alone.
Alone at last, she felt a girl again.

THOMAS LYNCH

Behold the Lilies of the Field

for Leonard Baskin

And now. An attempt.
Don't tense yourself; take it easy.
Look at the flowers there in the glass bowl.
Yes, they are lovely and fresh. I remember
Giving my mother flowers once, rather like those
(Are they narcissus or jonquils?)
And I hoped she would show some pleasure in them
But got that mechanical enthusiastic show
She used on the telephone once in praising some friend
For thoughtfulness or good taste or whatever it was,
And when she hung up, turned to us all and said,
'God, what a bore she is!'
I think she was trying to show us how honest she was,
At least with us. But the effect
Was just the opposite, and now I don't think
She knows what honesty is. 'Your mother's a whore,'
Someone said, not meaning she slept around,
Though perhaps this was part of it, but
Meaning she had lost all sense of honor,
And I think this is true.

But that's not what I wanted to say.
What was it I wanted to say?
When he said that about Mother, I had to laugh,
I really did, it was so amazingly true.
Where was I?
Lie back. Relax.
Oh yes. I remember now what it was.
It was what I saw them do to the emperor.
They captured him, you know. Eagles and all.
They stripped him, and made an iron collar for his neck,
And they made a cage out of our captured spears,
And they put him inside, naked and collared,

And exposed to the view of the whole enemy camp.
And I was tied to a post and made to watch
When he was taken out and flogged by one of their generals
And then forced to offer his ripped back
As a mounting block for the barbarian king
To get on his horse;
And one time to get down on all fours to be the royal throne
When the king received our ambassadors
To discuss the question of ransom.
Of course, he didn't want ransom.
And I was tied to a post and made to watch.
That's enough for now. Lie back. Try to relax.
No, that's not all.
They kept it up for two months.
We were taken to their outmost provinces.
It was always the same, and we were always made to watch,
The others and I. How he stood it, I don't know.
And then suddenly
There were no more floggings or humiliations,
The king's personal doctor saw to his back,
He was given decent clothing, and the collar was taken off,
And they treated us all with a special courtesy.
By the time we reached their capital city
His back was completely healed.
They had taken the cage apart—
But of course they didn't give us back our spears.
Then later that month, it was a warm afternoon in May,
The rest of us were marched out to the central square.
The crowds were there already, and the posts were set up,
To which we were tied in the old watching positions.
And he was brought out in the old way, and stripped,
And then tied flat on a big rectangular table
So that only his head could move.
Then the king made a short speech to the crowds,
To which they responded with gasps of wild excitement,
And which was then translated for the rest of us.

It was the sentence. He was to be flayed alive,
As slowly as possible, to drag out the pain.
And we were made to watch. The king's personal doctor,
The one who had tended his back,
Came forward with a tray of surgical knives.
They began at the feet.
And we were not allowed to close our eyes
Or to look away. When they were done, hours later,
The skin was turned over to one of their saddle-makers
To be tanned and stuffed and sewn. And for what?
A hideous life-sized doll, filled out with straw,
In the skin of the Roman Emperor, Valerian,
With blanks of mother-of-pearl under the eyelids,
And painted shells that had been prepared beforehand
For the fingernails and toenails,
Roughly cross-stitched on the inseam of the legs
And up the back to the center of the head,
Swung in the wind on a rope from the palace flag-pole;
And young girls were brought there by their mothers
To be told about the male anatomy.
His death had taken hours.
They were very patient.
And with him passed away the honor of Rome.

In the end, I was ransomed. Mother paid for me.
You must rest now. You must. Lean back.
Look at the flowers.
Yes. I am looking. I wish I could be like them.

ANTHONY HECHT

Ye haue heard this yarn afore

(but I'm minded on it againe
thefe daies of fqualls and rank clouds
and raines as is uitriolic –

pines fhorn ftark as mizzen-mafts
wi neuer a frolicfome fowl –
and ye top-gallant air all rent):

how we was one Monday anchored
off Mafcarenhas Iflande
in fourteen fathom o water;
how, feeking diuerfion, we landed;
how, on ye trees, there was pigeons
as blue as polifhed flate
which fuffered vs, being fo tame,
for to pluck em iuft like fruits
from ye branches and pull their necks;
how we killed two hundred firft day;
how we alfo killed grey paraquets
(moft entertayninge to cetch
a grey paraquet and *twift* it
fo as it fqueals aloud
till ye reft of its kind flock round,
therevpon themfelues being cetched);
how there was alfo penguins
(which laft hath but ftumps for wings,
fo being ye eafier to kill)
which we killed above four hundred;
how there was alfo wild geefe
and turtles above an hundred;
how we killed all thefe and more;
and ye Tuefday more and more;
and ye Wednefday more and more;
and ye Thurfday more and more;
ye haue heard this yarn afore

PETER READING

Crusoe in England

A new volcano has erupted,
the papers say, and last week I was reading
where some ship saw an island being born:
at first a breath of steam, ten miles away;
and then a black fleck – basalt, probably –
rose in the mate's binoculars
and caught on the horizon like a fly.
They named it. But my poor old island's still
un-rediscovered, un-renamable.
None of the books has ever got it right.

Well, I had fifty-two
miserable, small volcanoes I could climb
with a few slithery strides –
volcanoes dead as ash heaps.
I used to sit on the edge of the highest one
and count the others standing up,
naked and leaden, with their heads blown off.
I'd think that if they were the size
I thought volcanoes should be, then I had
become a giant;
and if I had become a giant,
I couldn't bear to think what size
the goats and turtles were,
or the gulls, or the over-lapping rollers
– a glittering hexagon of rollers
closing and closing in, but never quite,
glittering and glittering, though the sky
was mostly overcast.

My island seemed to be
a sort of cloud-dump. All the hemisphere's
left-over clouds arrived and hung
above the craters – their parched throats
were hot to touch.

Was that why it rained so much?
And why sometimes the whole place hissed?
The turtles lumbered by, high-domed,
hissing like teakettles.
(And I'd have given years, or taken a few,
for any sort of kettle, of course.)
The folds of lava, running out to sea,
would hiss. I'd turn. And then they'd prove
to be more turtles.
The beaches were all lava, variegated,
black, red, and white, and gray;
the marbled colors made a fine display.
And I had waterspouts. Oh,
half a dozen at a time, far out,
they'd come and go, advancing and retreating,
their heads in cloud, their feet in moving patches
of scuffed-up white.
Glass chimneys, flexible, attenuated,
sacerdotal beings of glass . . . I watched
the water spiral up in them like smoke.
Beautiful, yes, but not much company.

I often gave way to self-pity.
'Do I deserve this? I suppose I must.
I wouldn't be here otherwise. Was there
a moment when I actually chose this?
I don't remember, but there could have been.'
What's wrong about self-pity, anyway?
With my legs dangling down familiarly
over a crater's edge, I told myself
'Pity should begin at home.' So the more
pity I felt, the more I felt at home.

The sun set in the sea; the same odd sun
rose from the sea,
and there was one of it and one of me.
The island had one kind of everything:

one tree snail, a bright violet-blue
with a thin shell, crept over everything,
over the one variety of tree,
a sooty, scrub affair.
Snail shells lay under these in drifts
and, at a distance,
you'd swear that they were beds of irises.
There was one kind of berry, a dark red.
I tried it, one by one, and hours apart.
Sub-acid, and not bad, no ill effects;
and so I made home-brew. I'd drink
the awful, fizzy, stinging stuff
that went straight to my head
and play my home-made flute
(I think it had the weirdest scale on earth)
and, dizzy, whoop and dance among the goats.
Home-made, home-made! But aren't we all?
I felt a deep affection for
the smallest of my island industries.
No, not exactly, since the smallest was
a miserable philosophy.

Because I didn't know enough.
Why didn't I know enough of something?
Greek drama or astronomy? The books
I'd read were full of blanks;
the poems – well, I tried
reciting to my iris-beds,
'They flash upon that inward eye,
which is the bliss...' The bliss of what?
One of the first things that I did
when I got back was look it up.

The island smelled of goat and guano.
The goats were white, so were the gulls,
and both too tame, or else they thought
I was a goat, too, or a gull.

Baa, baa, baa and *shriek, shriek, shriek,*
baa ... shriek ... baa ... I still can't shake
them from my ears; they're hurting now.
The questioning shrieks, the equivocal replies
over a ground of hissing rain
and hissing, ambulating turtles
got on my nerves.

When all the gulls flew up at once, they sounded
like a big tree in a strong wind, its leaves.
I'd shut my eyes and think about a tree,
an oak, say, with real shade, somewhere.
I'd heard of cattle getting island-sick.
I thought the goats were.
One billy-goat would stand on the volcano
I'd christened *Mont d'Espoir* or *Mount Despair*
(I'd time enough to play with names),
and bleat and bleat, and sniff the air.
I'd grab his beard and look at him.
His pupils, horizontal, narrowed up
and expressed nothing, or a little malice.
I got so tired of the very colors!
One day I dyed a baby goat bright red
with my red berries, just to see
something a little different.
And then his mother wouldn't recognize him.

Dreams were the worst. Of course I dreamed of food
and love, but they were pleasant rather
than otherwise. But then I'd dream of things
like slitting a baby's throat, mistaking it
for a baby goat. I'd have
nightmares of other islands
stretching away from mine, infinities
of islands, islands spawning islands,
like frogs' eggs turning into polliwogs
of islands, knowing that I had to live

on each and every one, eventually,
for ages, registering their flora,
their fauna, their geography.

Just when I thought I couldn't stand it
another minute longer, Friday came.
(Accounts of that have everything all wrong.)
Friday was nice.
Friday was nice, and we were friends.
If only he had been a woman!
I wanted to propagate my kind,
and so did he, I think, poor boy.
He'd pet the baby goats sometimes,
and race with them, or carry one around.
–Pretty to watch; he had a pretty body.

And then one day they came and took us off.

Now I live here, another island,
that doesn't seem like one, but who decides?
My blood was full of them; my brain
bred islands. But that archipelago
has petered out. I'm old.
I'm bored, too, drinking my real tea,
surrounded by uninteresting lumber.
The knife there on the shelf –
it reeked of meaning, like a crucifix.
It lived. How many years did I
beg it, implore it, not to break?
I knew each nick and scratch by heart,
the bluish blade, the broken tip,
the lines of wood-grain on the handle...
Now it won't look at me at all.
The living soul has dribbled away.
My eyes rest on it and pass on.

The local museum's asked me to
leave everything to them:

the flute, the knife, the shrivelled shoes,
my shedding goatskin trousers
(moths have got in the fur),
the parasol that took me such a time
remembering the way the ribs should go.
It still will work but, folded up,
looks like a plucked and skinny fowl.
How can anyone want such things?
– And Friday, my dear Friday, died of measles
seventeen years ago come March.

ELIZABETH BISHOP

Moon Landing

It's natural the Boys should whoop it up for
so huge a phallic triumph, an adventure
    it would not have occurred to women
      to think worth while, made possible only

because we like huddling in gangs and knowing
the exact time: yes, our sex may in fairness
    hurrah the deed, although the motives
      that primed it were somewhat less than *menschlich*.

A grand gesture. But what does it period?
What does it osse? We were always adroiter
    with objects than lives, and more facile
      at courage than kindness: from the moment

the first flint was flaked this landing was merely
a matter of time. But our selves, like Adam's,
    still don't fit us exactly, modern
      only in this – our lack of decorum.

Homer's heroes were certainly no braver
than our Trio, but more fortunate: Hector

was excused the insult of having
his valor covered by television.

Worth *going* to see? I can well believe it.
Worth *seeing*? Mneh! I once rode through a desert
and was not charmed: give me a watered
lively garden, remote from blatherers

about the New, the von Brauns and their ilk, where
on August mornings I can count the morning
glories, where to die has a meaning,
and no engine can shift my perspective.

Unsmudged, thank God, my Moon still queens the Heavens
as She ebbs and fulls, a Presence to glop at,
Her Old Man, made of grit not protein,
still visits my Austrian several

with His old detachment, and the old warnings
still have power to scare me: Hybris comes to
an ugly finish, Irreverence
is a greater oaf than Superstition.

Our apparatniks will continue making
the usual squalid mess called History:
all we can pray for is that artists,
chefs and saints may still appear to blithe it.

W. H. AUDEN

Landing on the Moon

Gobble the news with seven grains
of alligator pepper, a pinch of salt,
white chalk, one sea-deep cry
for man's hike to Jehovah-hood, or,
must we not submerge in rituals
this explosive moment of animal triumph?—

Catch my hand, brother
we are annexing the kingdom of the gods.

ODIA OFEIMUN

Outward

The staff slips from the hand
Hissing and swims on the polished floor.
It glides away to the desert.

It floats like a bird or lily
On the waves, to the ones who are arriving.
And if no god arrives,

Then everything yearns outward.
The honeycomb cell brims over
And the atom is broken in light.

Machines have made their god. They walk or fly.
The towers bend like Magi, mountains weep,
Needles go mad, and metal sheds a tear.

*

The astronaut is lifted
Away from the world, and drifts.
How easy it is to be there!

How easy to be anyone, anything but oneself!
The metal of the plane is breathing;
Sinuously it swims through the stars.

LOUIS SIMPSON

The Painter

Sitting between the sea and the buildings
He enjoyed painting the sea's portrait.
But just as children imagine a prayer
Is merely silence, he expected his subject
To rush up the sand, and, seizing a brush,
Plaster its own portrait on the canvas.

So there was never any paint on his canvas
Until the people who lived in the buildings
Put him to work: 'Try using the brush
As a means to an end. Select, for a portrait,
Something less angry and large, and more subject
To a painter's moods, or, perhaps, to a prayer.'

How could he explain to them his prayer
That nature, not art, might usurp the canvas?
He chose his wife for a new subject,
Making her vast, like ruined buildings,
As if, forgetting itself, the portrait
Had expressed itself without a brush.

Slightly encouraged, he dipped his brush
In the sea, murmuring a heartfelt prayer:
'My soul, when I paint this next portrait
Let it be you who wrecks the canvas.'
The news spread like wildfire through the buildings:
He had gone back to the sea for his subject.

Imagine a painter crucified by his subject!
Too exhausted even to lift his brush,
He provoked some artists leaning from the buildings
To malicious mirth: 'We haven't a prayer
Now, of putting ourselves on canvas,
Or getting the sea to sit for a portrait!'

Others declared it a self-portrait.
Finally all indications of a subject
Began to fade, leaving the canvas
Perfectly white. He put down the brush.
At once a howl, that was also a prayer,
Arose from the overcrowded buildings.

They tossed him, the portrait, from the tallest of the buildings;
And the sea devoured the canvas and the brush
As though his subject had decided to remain a prayer.

JOHN ASHBERY

The Lost Pilot

for my father, 1922–1944

Your face did not rot
like the others – the co-pilot,
for example, I saw him

yesterday. His face is corn-
mush: his wife and daughter,
the poor ignorant people, stare

as if he will compose soon.
He was more wronged than Job.
But your face did not rot

like the others – it grew dark,
and hard like ebony;
the features progressed in their

distinction. If I could cajole
you to come back for an evening,
down from your compulsive

orbiting, I would touch you,
read your face as Dallas,
your hoodlum gunner, now,

with the blistered eyes, reads
his braille editions. I would
touch your face as a disinterested

scholar touches an original page.
However frightening, I would
discover you, and I would not

turn you in; I would not make
you face your wife, or Dallas,
or the co-pilot, Jim. You

could return to your crazy
orbiting, and I would not try
to fully understand what

it means to you. All I know
is this: when I see you,
as I have seen you at least

once every year of my life,
spin across the wilds of the sky
like a tiny, African god,

I feel dead. I feel as if I were
the residue of a stranger's life,
that I should pursue you.

My head cocked toward the sky,
I cannot get off the ground,
and, you, passing over again,

fast, perfect, and unwilling
to tell me that you are doing
well, or that it was mistake

that placed you in that world,
and me in this; or that misfortune
placed these worlds in us.

JAMES TATE

Skywriting

Cool, clear autumn morning, so still
the knock of someone hammering
a nail rebounds from the floor
of the valley, with its shimmering

metal rivulets: that shadowy
vale in fact is a railway yard.
For some reason, on a Sunday,
a jet pilot has expelled a hard

stream of smoke behind his aircraft,
so precisely outlined
it could almost be a steel rail.
It's chilly, and there's no sigh of wind.

Flying high and fast, the pilot
has drawn a straight line, an arrow
of exhaust from one horizon
to the other, a path whose narrow

course is seen from the ground as curved,
so that it appears an enormous
basket-handle has been attached
to the land. Unlike the mischievous

Air Force trainee who, in the skies
over Perth, etched out in smoke form
his own private parts, as if he were
a vandal on a railway platform,

this pilot has not diverted
himself, leaving a colourless
rainbow arched over the city,
and over those suburban palaces

secured by the Bank. A rainbow,
though, is never as wide an arc
as the flowery canopy stretched
there now, like an archway in the park

arranged for a wedding. Beneath
its bridal bower, an airliner
coming in low resembles
a clumsy groom, cutting it finer

than he should, arrived with buttons
unfastened. An unhappy man
in Melbourne years ago rented
a skywriter, in desperation,

to advertise for a wife: people
always look at the sky. The track
made by this morning's jet may be
a less intricate message, yet its lack

is not of import: its simple
curve is the curve of the face
of the world, and hence it implies
all things within its embrace.

Like the world, the smoke meridian decays
before your eyes. Out of vision
an engine roar persists, sounding
like a far-distant storm's reverberation,

and like the football crowd I heard
once in a garden, a commotion
which could only be accounted for
as the shimmering pulse of the ocean.

JAMIE GRANT

[93]

Quiet Nights

I go to sleep on one beach,
wake up on another.
Boat all fitted out,
tugging against its rope.

RAYMOND CARVER

Lives

for Seamus Heaney

First time out
I was a torc of gold
And wept tears of the sun.

That was fun
But they buried me
In the earth two thousand years

Till a labourer
Turned me up with a pick
In eighteen fifty-four

And sold me
For tea and sugar
In Newmarket-on-Fergus.

Once I was an oar
But stuck in the shore
To mark the place of a grave

When the lost ship
Sailed away. I thought
Of Ithaca, but soon decayed.

The time that I liked
Best was when
I was a bump of clay

In a Navaho rug,
Put there to mitigate
The too godlike

Perfection of that
Merely human artifact.
I served my maker well—

He lived long
To be struck down in
Tucson by an electric shock

The night the lights
Went out in Europe
Never to shine again.

So many lives,
So many things to remember!
I was a stone in Tibet,

A tongue of bark
At the heart of Africa
Growing darker and darker...

It all seems
A little unreal now,
Now that I am

An anthropologist
With my own
Credit card, dictaphone,

Army surplus boots,
And a whole boatload
Of photographic equipment.

I know too much
To be anything any more;
And if in the distant

Future someone
Thinks he has once been me
As I am today,

Let him revise
His insolent ontology
Or teach himself to pray.

DEREK MAHON

The Red Judge

We shut the red judge in a bronze jar
– By 'we', meaning myself and the black judge –
And there was peace, for a time. You can have enough
Yowling from certain justices. The jar
We buried, (pitching and swelling like the tough
Membrane of an unshelled egg), on the Calton Hill.
And there was peace, for a time. My friend the black
Judge was keen on whisky, and I kept
Within earshot of sobriety only by drinking
Slow ciders, and pretending
Unfelt absorption in the repetitive beer-mats. It was a kind of
Vibration we noticed first – hard to tell
Whether we heard it or were shaken by,
Whether the tumblers quivered or our minds. It grew
To a thick thudding, and an occasional creak
Like a nearby axle, but as it were
Without the sense of 'nearby'. – The hard flag-
stones wriggled slightly under the taut linoleum.
I supported the black judge to the nearest door
– Detached his clutched glass for the protesting barman –

And propped him against a bus-stop. Maybe
It was only a pneumatic drill mating at Queen Street,
Or an impotent motor-bike – the sounds grew harsher.
My gestures stopped a 24 that spat
Some eleventh commandment out of its sober driver,
But I was more conscious of the rocking walls,
The pavement's shrugging off its granite kerb...

Quite suddenly the night was still: the cracks
In the roadway rested, and the tenements
Of Rose Street stood inscrutable as always. The black judge
Snored at his post. And all around
The bright blood filled the gutters, overflowed
The window-sills and doorsteps, soaked my anyway
Inadequate shoes, and there was a sound of cheering
Faintly and everywhere, and the Red Judge walked
O thirty feet high and scarlet towards our stop.

D. M. BLACK

The Video Box: 25

If you ask what my favourite programme is
it has to be that strange world jigsaw final.
After the winner had defeated all his rivals
with harder and harder jigsaws, he had to prove his mettle
by completing one last absolute mindcrusher
on his own, under the cameras, in less than a week.
We saw, but he did not, what the picture would be:
the mid-Atlantic, photographed from a plane,
as featureless a stretch as could be found,
no weeds, no flotsam, no birds, no oil, no ships,
the surface neither stormy nor calm, but ordinary,
a light wind on a slowly rolling swell.
Hand-cut by a fiendish jigger to simulate,
but not to have, identical beaks and bays,

it seemed impossible; but the candidate—
he said he was a stateless person, called himself Smith—
was impressive: small, dark, nimble, self-contained.
The thousands of little grey tortoises were scattered
on the floor of the studio; we saw the clock; he started.
His food was brought to him, but he hardly ate.
He had a bed, with the light only dimmed to a weird blue,
never out. By the first day he had established
the edges, saw the picture was three metres long
and appeared to represent (dear God!) the sea.
Well, it was a man's life, and the silence
(broken only by sighs, click of wood, plop of coffee
in paper cups) that kept me fascinated.
Even when one hand was picking the edge-pieces
I noticed his other hand was massing sets
of distinguishing ripples or darker cross-hatching or
incipient wave-crests; his mind,
if not his face, worked like a sea.
It was when he suddenly rose from his bed
at two, on the third night, went straight over
to one piece and slotted it into a growing central patch,
then back to bed, that I knew he would make it.
On the sixth day he looked haggard and slow,
with perhaps a hundred pieces left,
of the most dreary unmarked lifeless grey.
The camera showed the clock more frequently.
He roused himself, and in a quickening burst
of activity, with many false starts, began
to press that inhuman insolent remnant together.
He did it, on the evening of the sixth day.
People streamed onto the set. Bands played.
That was fine. But what I liked best
was the last shot of the completed sea,
filling the screen; then the saw-lines disappeared,
till almost imperceptibly the surface moved
and it was again the real Atlantic, glad

to distraction to be released, raised
above itself in growing gusts, allowed
to roar as rain drove down and darkened,
allowed to blot, for a moment, the orderer's hand.

EDWIN MORGAN

Lighthouse

That night the house
Troubled the householder's sleep
And became a kind of Wolf Rock.

What was the loft was
Where the precious light burned,
And the slates of a tough

Roof turned transparent
And prismatic, focusing
That warm, floating lantern's glow.

An ordinary suburbia
Changed to black, frightening sea,
And everything was round;

Rooms, windows, eyes
As he found his stairs
Went down further

Than there were before floors.
His front door seemed
At the base of a well

As he turned the starfish
Handle and stepped
Into the kelp and shells

Of a one-time front garden
And saw the proof, his house
A tower striped like crockery

Occulting its name
Across hostile brine,
Occurring in the Admiralty

Lists of Lights,
Brother to Bishop Rock,
Friend of Eddystone, ancient

As Pharos, he felt proud,
He saw the ships lit up and safe,
He heard the living captains hailing.

GERARD WOODWARD

Popular Mechanics

The enormous engineering problems
You'll encounter by attempting to crucify yourself
Without helpers, pulleys, cogwheels,
And other clever mechanical contrivances—

In a small, bare, white room,
With only a loose-legged chair
To reach the height of the ceiling—
Only a shoe to beat the nails in.

Not to mention being naked for the occasion—
So that each rib and muscle shows.
Your left hand already spiked in,
Only the right to wipe the sweat with,

To help yourself to a butt
From the overflowed ashtray,

You won't quite manage to light –
And the night coming, the whiz night.

CHARLES SIMIC

Always

for Charles Simic

Always so late in the day
In their rumpled clothes, sitting
Around a table lit by a single bulb,
The great forgetters were hard at work.
They tilted their heads to one side, closing their eyes.
Then a house disappeared, and a man in his yard
With all his flowers in a row.
The great forgetters wrinkled their brows.
Then Florida went and San Francisco
Where tugs and barges leave
Small gleaming scars across the Bay.
One of the great forgetters struck a match.
Gone were the harps of beaded lights
That vault the rivers of New York.
Another filled his glass
And that was it for crowds at evening
Under sulphur yellow streetlamps coming on.
And afterwards Bulgaria was gone, and then Japan.
'Where will it stop?' one of them said.
'Such difficult work, pursuing the fate
Of everything known,' said another.
'Down to the last stone,' said a third,
'And only the cold zero of perfection
Left for the imagination.' And gone
Were North and South America,
And gone as well the moon.
Another yawned, another gazed at the window:

No grass, no trees...
The blaze of promise everywhere.

MARK STRAND

I Am a Finn

I am standing in the post office, about
to mail a package back to Minnesota, to my family.
I am a Finn. My name is Kasteheimi (Dewdrop).

Mikael Agricola (1510–1557) created the Finnish language.
He knew Luther and translated the New Testament.
When I stop by the Classé Café for a cheeseburger

no one suspects that I am a Finn.
I gaze at the dimestore reproductions of Lautrec
on the greasy walls, at the punk lovers afraid

to show their quivery emotions, secure
in the knowledge that my grandparents really did
emigrate from Finland in 1910 – why

is everybody leaving Finland, hundreds of
thousands to Michigan and Minnesota, and now Australia?
Eighty-six percent of Finnish men have blue

or grey eyes. Today is Charlie Chaplin's
one hundredth birthday, though he is not
Finnish or alive: 'Thy blossom, in the bud

laid low.' The commonest fur-bearing animals
are the red squirrel, musk-rat, pine-marten
and fox. There are about 35,000 elk.

But I should be studying for my exam.
I wonder if Dean will celebrate with me tonight,
assuming I pass. Finnish literature

really came alive in the 1860s.
Here, in Cambridge, Massachusetts,
no one cares that I am a Finn.

They've never even heard of Frans Eemil Sillanpää,
winner of the 1939 Nobel Prize in Literature.
As a Finn, this infuriates me.

JAMES TATE

I Am Still a Finn

I failed my exam, which is difficult
for me to understand because I am a Finn.
We are a bright, if slightly depressed, people.

Pertti Palmroth is the strongest name
in Finnish footwear design; his shoes and boots
are exported to seventeen countries.

Dean bought champagne to celebrate
my failure. He says I was just nervous.
Between 1908 and 1950, 33 volumes

of *The Ancient Poetry of the Finnish People*
were issued, the largest work of its kind
ever published in any language.

So why should I be nervous? Aren't I
a Finn, descendent of Johan Ludvig Runeberg
(1804–1877), Finnish national poet?

I know he wrote in Swedish, and this
depresses me still. Harvard Square
is never 'empty'. There is no chance

that I will ever be able to state honestly
that 'Harvard Square is empty tonight.'
A man from Nigeria will be opening

his umbrella, and a girl from Wyoming
will be closing hers. A Zulu warrior
is running to catch a bus and an over-

painted harlot from Buenos Aires will
be fainting on schedule. And I, a Finn,
will long for the dwarf birches of the north

I have never seen. For 73 days the sun
never sinks below the horizon. O
darkness, mine! I shall always be a Finn.

JAMES TATE

Consolation

I came back from home yesterday, spent
the old, dreary leave routine.
Father was lying in bed, and I said:
'Don't die yet. You know the funerals these days.'
'The last I attended was so foul I felt
like not dying, with civil service children,' he said.
'And that's what I mean. Don't die.'
He declined the naira notes I stretched before him,
not looking at them. Colours mattered not to him.
'Save. Nobody knows when this tree will fall;
the winds are out to do damage
with these unending fevers. Son, save.'
And there he was, consoled by my visit,
believing that what didn't go to him
would not get lost elsewhere.
We've never been really as close as now, since
my mother left him after I went to school.
Come to think of it, the old man is playing
a trick on me – asking me to visit from far
and turning down my offers, not needy

in indigence. He lives longer, self-supported.
And I end up in a roadside bar cracking bottles,
learning the game of wake-keeping, when
I'll have to go out of myself to swim in *Schnapps*
performing my duties as the first son
of a considerate proud tortoise.

TANURE OJAIDE

The Turtle

for my grandson

Not because of his eyes,
        the eyes of a bird,
                but because he is beaked,
birdlike, to do an injury,
        has the turtle attracted you.
                He is your only pet.
When we are together
        you talk of nothing else
                ascribing all sorts
of murderous motives
        to his least action.
                You ask me
to write a poem,
        should I have poems to write,
                about a turtle.
The turtle lives in the mud
        but is not mud-like,
                you can tell it by his eyes
which are clear.
        When he shall escape
                his present confinement

he will stride about the world
                    destroying all
                                with his sharp beak.
Whatever opposes him
                    in the streets of the city
                                shall go down.
Cars will be overturned.
                    And upon his back
                                shall ride,
to his conquests,
                    my Lord,
                                you!

You shall be master!
                    In the beginning
                                there was a great tortoise
who supported the world.
                    Upon him
                                all ultimately
rests.
                    Without him
                                nothing will stand.
He is all wise
                    and can outrun the hare.
                                In the night
his eyes carry him
                    to unknown places.
                                He is your friend.

WILLIAM CARLOS WILLIAMS

The Fish in the Stone

The fish in the stone
would like to fall
back into the sea.

He is weary
of analysis, the small
predictable truths.
He is weary of waiting
in the open,
his profile stamped
by a white light.

In the ocean the silence
moves and moves

and so much is unnecessary!
Patient, he drifts
until the moment comes
to cast his
skeletal blossom.

The fish in the stone
knows to fail is
to do the living
a favor.

He knows why the ant
engineers a gangster's
funeral, garish
and perfectly amber.
He knows why the scientist
in secret delight
strokes the fern's
voluptuous braille.

    RITA DOVE

The Sea Eats the Land at Home

At home the sea is in the town,
Running in and out of the cooking places,
Collecting the firewood from the hearths
And sending it back at night;
The sea eats the land at home.
It came one day at the dead of night,
Destroying the cement walls,
And carried away the fowls,
The cooking-pots and the ladles,
The sea eats the land at home;
It is a sad thing to hear the wails,
And the mourning shouts of the women,
Calling on all the gods they worship,
To protect them from the angry sea.
Aku stood outside where her cooking-pot stood,
With her two children shivering from the cold,
Her hands on her breast,
Weeping mournfully.
Her ancestors have neglected her,
Her gods have deserted her,
It was a cold Sunday morning,
The storm was raging,
Goats and fowls were struggling in the water,
The angry water of the cruel sea;
The lap-lapping of the bark water at the shore,
And above the sobs and the deep and low moans
Was the eternal hum of the living sea.
It has taken away their belongings,
Adena has lost the trinkets which
Were her dowry and her joy
In the sea that eats the land at home,
Eats the whole land at home.

GEORGE AWOONOR-WILLIAMS

Meeting the British

We met the British in the dead of winter.
The sky was lavender

and the snow lavender-blue.
I could hear, far below,

the sound of two streams coming together
(both were frozen over)

and, no less strange,
myself calling out in French

across that forest-
clearing. Neither General Jeffrey Amherst

nor Colonel Henry Bouquet
could stomach our willow-tobacco.

As for the unusual
scent when the Colonel shook out his hand-

kerchief: *C'est la lavande,*
une fleur mauve comme le ciel.

They gave us six fishhooks
and two blankets embroidered with smallpox.

PAUL MULDOON

In the Country of the Black Pig

Wet, this is instantly mud country, and then as suddenly
dust again; the sun comes out to show how the floods push
whole river-beds into the sweltering bay. The wild, black pigs
are a terror, barrelling out of the coarse green bush

and stampeding down the main street, cutting across
the traffic in the town which shrinks, like an old man, unwell
and deaf in one ear, always inclining towards its neglected
port, the undredged harbour silting up, a choking shell.

The pigs seem to go dancing on the perfect beach:
not far from here the *Grosvenor* drowned in all its gold.
The future fattens on the terrible rumour that the pigs
will snatch a great treasure from the rotten hold.

The settlers are leaving and the pigs grow even bolder;
unmoved by exploding aerosols, they make mad bombing runs
among the bulging, smoking dust-bins. In the church porch
a pregnant sow shows her brilliant teeth. Children carry guns.

A few stay on, tending the cemetery on the hill, their gift
of a cannon in Soldiers' Corner defends the honoured bones.
They'll be safe enough here, we say, as if these graves
were primed and waiting shells, an arsenal of headstones.

Everyone says beyond the town lies freedom, a new hinterland
but difficult to identify because its name is changing constantly.
You are Leaving the Official Zone the warning signs proclaim.
On the road out of town a black pig has been nailed to a tree.

CHRISTOPHER HOPE

Shame

It is a cramped little state with no foreign policy,
Save to be thought inoffensive. The grammar of the language
Has never been fathomed, owing to the national habit
Of allowing each sentence to trail off in confusion.
Those who have visited Scusi, the capital city,
Report that the railway-route from Schuldig passes
Through country best described as unrelieved.
Sheep are the national product. The faint inscription

Over the city gates may perhaps be rendered,
'I'm afraid you won't find much of interest here.'
Census-reports which give the population
As zero are, of course, not to be trusted,
Save as reflecting the natives' flustered insistence
That they do not count, as well as their modest horror
Of letting one's sex be known in so many words.
The uniform grey of the nondescript buildings, the absence
Of churches or comfort-stations, have given observers
An odd impression of ostentatious meanness,
And it must be said of the citizens (muttering by
In their ratty sheepskins, shying at cracks in the sidewalk)
That they lack the peace of mind of the truly humble.
The tenor of life is careful, even in the stiff
Unsmiling carelessness of the border-guards
And *douaniers*, who admit, whenever they can,
Not merely the usual carloads of deodorant
But gypsies, g-strings, hasheesh, and contraband pigments.
Their complete negligence is reserved, however,
For the hoped-for invasion, at which time the happy people
(Sniggering, ruddily naked, and shamelessly drunk)
Will stun the foe by their overwhelming submission,
Corrupt the generals, infiltrate the staff,
Usurp the throne, proclaim themselves to be sun-gods,
And bring about the collapse of the whole empire.

RICHARD WILBUR

The Applicant

First, are you our sort of a person?
Do you wear
A glass eye, false teeth or a crutch,
A brace or a hook,
Rubber breasts or a rubber crotch,

Stitches to show something's missing? No, no? Then
How can we give you a thing?
Stop crying.
Open your hand.
Empty? Empty. Here is a hand

To fill it and willing
To bring teacups and roll away headaches
And do whatever you tell it.
Will you marry it?
It is guaranteed

To thumb shut your eyes at the end
And dissolve of sorrow.
We make new stock from the salt.
I notice you are stark naked.
How about this suit—

Black and stiff, but not a bad fit.
Will you marry it?
It is waterproof, shatterproof, proof
Against fire and bombs through the roof.
Believe me, they'll bury you in it.

Now your head, excuse me, is empty.
I have the ticket for that.
Come here, sweetie, out of the closet.
Well, what do you think of *that*?
Naked as paper to start

But in twenty-five years she'll be silver,
In fifty, gold.
A living doll, everywhere you look.
It can sew, it can cook,
It can talk, talk, talk.

It works, there is nothing wrong with it.
You have a hole, it's a poultice.
You have an eye, it's an image.

My boy, it's your last resort.
Will you marry it, marry it, marry it.

SYLVIA PLATH

Black March

I have a friend
At the end
Of the world.
His name is a breath

Of fresh air.
He is dressed in
Grey chiffon. At least
I think it is chiffon.
It has a
Peculiar look, like smoke.

It wraps him round
It blows out of place
It conceals him
I have not seen his face.

But I have seen his eyes, they are
As pretty and bright
As raindrops on black twigs
In March, and heard him say:

I am a breath
Of fresh air for you, a change
By and by.

Black March I call him
Because of his eyes
Being like March raindrops
On black twigs.

(Such a pretty time when the sky
Behind black twigs can be seen
Stretched out in one
Uninterrupted
Cambridge blue as cold as snow.)

But this friend
Whatever new names I give him
Is an old friend. He says:

Whatever names you give me
I am
A breath of fresh air,
A change for you.

STEVIE SMITH

Badly-Chosen Lover

Criminal, you took a great piece of my life,
And you took it under false pretences,
That piece of time
– In the clear muscles of my brain
I have the lens and jug of it!
Books, thoughts, meals, days, and houses,
Half Europe, spent like a coarse banknote,
You took it – leaving mud and cabbage stumps.

And, Criminal, I damn you for it (very softly).
My spirit broke her fast on you. And, Turk,
You fed her with the breath of your neck
– In my brain's clear retina
I have the stolen love-behaviour.
Your heart, greedy and tepid, brothel-meat,
Gulped it, like a flunkey with erotica.
And very softly, Criminal, I *damn* you for it.

ROSEMARY TONKS

Hydromaniac

I was leaning across your chest;
Like a marble-smith, I made pencilmarks over
Its vanilla skin, its young man's skin,
Refreshing as the pleasure page in a daily newspaper.
I sniffed you to quench my thirst,
As one sniffs in the sky huge, damp sheets of lightning
That bring down the chablis, hocks, moselles,
And tear cold, watery holes.
Those soaking wet chords from Brahms (... their overflow,
On which you could float a canoe)
Are not more refreshing! Nor is the fragrant gin-fizz
From the glass joint of a rod of grass.

My life cries out for water!
Haughty sheets of newsprint, lightning, music, skin!
Haughty bathrooms where the lukewarm swimmer
In his water-colour coat of soap is king.

ROSEMARY TONKS

My Shoes

Shoes, secret face of my inner life:
Two gaping toothless mouths,
Two partly decomposed animal skins
Smelling of mice-nests.

My brother and sister who died at birth
Continuing their existence in you,
Guiding my life
Toward their incomprehensible innocence.

What use are books to me
When in you it is possible to read

The Gospel of my life on earth
And still beyond, of things to come?

I want to proclaim the religion
I have devised for your perfect humility
And the strange church I am building
With you as the altar.

Ascetic and maternal, you endure:
Kin to oxen, to Saints, to condemned men,
With your mute patience, forming
The only true likeness of myself.

CHARLES SIMIC

Dream Songs

4

Filling her compact & delicious body
with chicken páprika, she glanced at me
twice.
Fainting with interest, I hungered back
and only the fact of her husband & four other people
kept me from springing on her

or falling at her little feet and crying
'You are the hottest one for years of night
Henry's dazed eyes
have enjoyed, Brilliance.' I advanced upon
(despairing) my spumoni. – Sir Bones: is stuffed,
de world, wif feeding girls.

– Black hair, complexion Latin, jewelled eyes
downcast ... The slob beside her   feasts ... What wonders is
she sitting on, over there?
The restaurant buzzes. She might as well be on Mars.

Where did it all go wrong? There ought to be a law against
    Henry.
– Mr Bones: there is.

63

Bats have no bankers and they do not drink
and cannot be arrested and pay no tax
and, in general, bats have it made.
Henry for joining the human race is *bats*,
known to be so, by few them who think,
out of the cave.

Instead of the cave! ah lovely-chilly, dark,
ur-moist his cousins hang in hundreds or swerve
with personal radar,
crisisless, kid. Instead of the cave? I serve,
inside, my blind term. Filthy four-foot lights
reflect on the whites of our eyes.

He then salutes for sixty years of it
just now a one of valor and insights,
a theatrical man,
O scholar & Legionnaire who as quickly might
have killed as cast you. *Olè*. Stormed with years
he tranquil commands and appears.

JOHN BERRYMAN

Henry by Night

Henry's nocturnal habits were the terror of his women.
First it appears he snored, lying on his back.
Then he thrashed & tossed,
changing position like a task fleet. Then, inhuman,
he woke every hour or so – they couldn't keep track
of mobile Henry, lost

at 3 a.m., off for more drugs or a cigarette,
reading old mail, writing new letters, scribbling
excessive Songs;
back then to bed, to the old tune or get set
for a stercoraceous cough, without quibbling
death-like. His women's wrongs

they hoarded & forgave, mysterious, sweet;
but you'll admit it was no way to live
or even keep alive.
I won't mention the dreams I won't repeat
sweating & shaking: something's gotta give:
up for good at five.

JOHN BERRYMAN

Memories of West Street and Lepke

Only teaching on Tuesdays, book-worming
in pajamas fresh from the washer each morning,
I hog a whole house on Boston's
'hardly passionate Marlborough Street',
where even the man
scavenging filth in the back alley trash cans,
has two children, a beach wagon, a helpmate,
and is a 'young Republican'.
I have a nine months' daughter,
young enough to be my granddaughter.
Like the sun she rises in her flame-flamingo infants' wear.

These are the tranquillized *Fifties*,
and I am forty. Ought I to regret my seedtime?
I was a fire-breathing Catholic C.O.,
and made my manic statement,
telling off the state and president, and then

sat waiting sentence in the bull pen
beside a Negro boy with curlicues
of marijuana in his hair.

Given a year,
I walked on the roof of the West Street Jail, a short
enclosure like my school soccer court,
and saw the Hudson River once a day
through sooty clothesline entanglements
and bleaching khaki tenements.
Strolling, I yammered metaphysics with Abramowitz,
a jaundice-yellow ('it's really tan')
and fly-weight pacifist,
so vegetarian,
he wore rope shoes and preferred fallen fruit.
He tried to convert Bioff and Brown,
the Hollywood pimps, to his diet.
Hairy, muscular, suburban,
wearing chocolate double-breasted suits,
they blew their tops and beat him black and blue.

I was so out of things, I'd never heard
of the Jehovah's Witnesses.
'Are you a C.O.?' I asked a fellow jailbird.
'No,' he answered, 'I'm a J.W.'
He taught me the 'hospital tuck',
and pointed out the T-shirted back
of *Murder Incorporated*'s Czar Lepke,
there piling towels on a rack,
or dawdling off to his little segregated cell full
of things forbidden the common man:
a portable radio, a dresser, two toy American
flags tied together with a ribbon of Easter palm.
Flabby, bald, lobotomized,
he drifted in a sheepish calm,
where no agonizing reappraisal

jarred his concentration on the electric chair—
hanging like an oasis in his air
of lost connections...

ROBERT LOWELL

The Bight

(*On my birthday*)

At low tide like this how sheer the water is.
White, crumbling ribs of marl protrude and glare
and the boats are dry, the pilings dry as matches.
Absorbing, rather than being absorbed,
the water in the bight doesn't wet anything,
the color of the gas flame turned as low as possible.
One can smell it turning to gas; if one were Baudelaire
one could probably hear it turning to marimba music.
The little ocher dredge at work off the end of the dock
already plays the dry perfectly off-beat claves.
The birds are outsize. Pelicans crash
into this peculiar gas unnecessarily hard,
it seems to me, like pickaxes,
rarely coming up with anything to show for it,
and going off with humorous elbowings.
Black-and-white man-of-war birds soar
on impalpable drafts
and open their tails like scissors on the curves
or tense them like wishbones, till they tremble.
The frowsy sponge boats keep coming in
with the obliging air of retrievers,
bristling with jackstraw gaffs and hooks
and decorated with bobbles of sponges.
There is a fence of chicken wire along the dock
where, glinting like little plowshares,
the blue-gray shark tails are hung up to dry

for the Chinese-restaurant trade.
Some of the little white boats are still piled up
against each other, or lie on their sides, stove in,
and not yet salvaged, if they ever will be, from the last bad
    storm,
like torn-open, unanswered letters.
The bight is littered with old correspondences.
Click. Click. Goes the dredge,
and brings up a dripping jawful of marl.
All the untidy activity continues,
awful but cheerful.

ELIZABETH BISHOP

Boat Poem

I wish there were a touch of these boats about my life;
so to speak, a tarring,
the touch of inspired disorder and something more than that,
something more too
than the mobility of sails or a primitive bumpy engine,
under that tiny hot-house window,
which eats up oil and benzine perhaps
but will go on beating in spite of the many strains
not needing with luck to be repaired too often,
with luck lasting years piled on years.

There must be a kind of envy which brings me peering
and nosing at the boats along the island quay
either in the hot morning
with the lace-light shaking up against their hulls from the
    water,
or when their mast-tops
keep on drawing lines between stars.
(I do not speak here of the private yachts from the clubs

which stalk across the harbour like magnificent white cats
but sheer off and keep mostly to themselves.)

Look for example at the Bartolomé; a deck-full
of mineral water and bottles of beer in cases
and great booming barrels of wine from the mainland,
endearing trade;
and lengths of timber and iron rods for building
and, curiously, a pig with flying ears
ramming a wet snout into whatever it explores.

Or the Virgen del Pilar, mantled and weavy with drooping nets
PM/708/3A
with starfish and pieces of cod drying on the wheel-house roof
some wine, the remains of supper on an enamel plate
and trousers and singlets 'passim';
both of these boats stinky and forgivable like some great men,
both needing paint,
but both, one observes, armoured far better than us against
    jolts
by a belt of old motor-tyres lobbed round their sides for
    buffers.

And having in their swerving planks and in the point of their
    bows
the never-enough-to-be-praised
authority of a great tradition, the sea-shape
simple and true like a vase,
something that stays too in the carved head of an eagle
or that white-eyed wooden hound crying up beneath the
    bowsprit.

Qualities clearly admirable. So is their response to occasion,
how they celebrate such times
and suddenly fountain with bunting and stand like ocean
    maypoles
on a Saint's Day when a gun bangs from the fortifications,
and an echo-gun throws a bang back

and all the old kitchen bells start hammering from the
    churches.

Admirable again
how one of them, perhaps tomorrow, will have gone with no
    hooting or fuss,
simply absent from its place among the others,
occupied, without self importance, in the thousands-of-millions-
    of sea.

BERNARD SPENCER

The Quality of Sprawl

Sprawl is the quality
of the man who cut down his Rolls Royce
into a farm utility truck, and sprawl
is what the company lacked when it made repeated efforts
to buy the vehicle back and repair its image.

Sprawl is doing your farming by aeroplane, roughly,
or driving a hitchhiker that extra hundred miles home.
It is the rococo of being your own still centre.
It is never lighting cigars with ten-dollar notes:
that's idiot ostentation and murder of starving people.
Nor can it be bought with the ash of million-dollar deeds.

Sprawl lengthens the legs; it trains greyhounds on liver and
    beer.
Sprawl almost never says Why not? with palms comically
    raised
nor can it be dressed for, not even in running shoes worn
with mink and a nose ring. That is Society. That's Style.
Sprawl is more like the thirteenth banana in a dozen
or anyway the fourteenth.

Sprawl is Hank Stamper in *Never Give an Inch*
bisecting an obstructive official's desk with a chain saw.
Not harming the official. Sprawl is never brutal
though it's often intransigent. Sprawl is never Simon de
    Montfort
at a town-storming: Kill them all! God will know his own.
Knowing the man's name this was said to might be sprawl.

Sprawl occurs in art. The fifteenth to twenty-first
lines in a sonnet, for example. And in certain paintings;
I have sprawl enough to have forgotten which paintings.
Turner's glorious Burning of the Houses of Parliament
comes to mind, a doubling bannered triumph of sprawl –
except, he didn't fire them.

Sprawl gets up the nose of many kinds of people
(every kind that comes in kinds) whose futures don't include it.
Some decry it as criminal presumption, silken-robed Pope
    Alexander
dividing the new world between Spain and Portugal.
If he smiled *in petto* afterwards, perhaps the thing did have
    sprawl.

Sprawl is really classless, though. It's John Christopher
    Frederick Murray
asleep in his neighbours' best bed in spurs and oilskins
but not having thrown up:
sprawl is never Calum who, in the loud hallway of our house,
reinvented the Festoon. Rather
it's Beatrice Miles going twelve hundred ditto in a taxi,
No Lewd Advances, No Hitting Animals, No Speeding,
on the proceeds of her two-bob-a-sonnet Shakespeare readings.
An image of my country. And would that it were more so.

No, sprawl is full-gloss murals on a council-house wall.
Sprawl leans on things. It is loose-limbed in its mind.
Reprimanded and dismissed
it listens with a grin and one boot up on the rail

of possibility. It may have to leave the Earth.
Being roughly Christian, it scratches the other cheek
and thinks it unlikely. Though people have been shot for sprawl.

LES MURRAY

The Monuments

Each year the monuments grew larger.
The citizens demanded this.
As their lives got worse they wanted
longer staircases to descend, towering fountains ...

Taxes were increased. A famine settled in.
An inexplicable epidemic appeared.
Autumn was rain-sodden. So,
they collected funds for a new work

in the form of a giant, granite pineapple
encircled by a narrow staircase,
so difficult to climb some said
it symbolized life or friendship.

The monuments meant nothing of course.
The misfortune seemed undeserved.
At parties the food was served
on plates in the form of clouds

that descended from the ceiling,
and under each unseasonal strawberry
a gold leaf was set. Despite these strategies
the general melancholy increased.

Poems concerned themselves
with childhood, autumn and failure,
although it was understood that these took the place
of events too unbearable to discuss.

Work resumed on the pineapple.
It was decided to enclose it within a transparent
sphere inscribed with a poem concerning
autumn and failure. Meanwhile

in the downtown area, work began on a new
staircase, some 900 feet high, leading to
a colossal weeping eye. On rainy days
citizens would gather to watch the way

it vanished sweetly into mist,
but no one dared to place a foot
on even the lowest, shining step:
'This is art,' they said, 'We cannot use it.'

JOHN ASH

A Low Temple

A low temple keeps its gods in the dark.
You lend a matchbox to the priest.
One by one the gods come to light.
Amused bronze. Smiling stone. Unsurprised.
For a moment the length of a matchstick
gesture after gesture revives and dies.
Stance after lost stance is found
and lost again.
Who was that, you ask.
The eight arm goddess, the priest replies.
A sceptic match coughs.
You can count.
But she has eighteen, you protest.
All the same she is still an eight arm goddess to the priest.
You come out in the sun and light a charminar.
Children play on the back of the twenty-foot tortoise.

ARUN KOLATKAR

The Empty Church

They laid this stone trap
for him, enticing him with candles,
as though he would come like some huge moth
out of the darkness to beat there.
Ah, he had burned himself
before in the human flame
and escaped, leaving the reason
torn. He will not come any more

to our lure. Why, then, do I kneel still
striking my prayers on a stone
heart? Is it in hope one
of them will ignite yet and throw
on its illumined walls the shadow
of someone greater than I can understand?

R. S. THOMAS

The God of Love

*The musk-ox is accustomed to near-Arctic conditions. When
danger threatens, these beasts cluster together to form a defensive
wall or a 'porcupine' with the calves in the middle.*
DR WOLFGANG ENGELHARDT, Survival of the Free

I found them between far hills, by a frozen lake.
    On a patch of bare ground. They were grouped
In a solid ring, like an ark of horn. And around
    Them circled, slowly closing in,
Their tongues lolling, their ears flattened against the wind,

    A whirlpool of wolves. As I breathed, one fragment of bone
      and
    Muscle detached itself from the mass and
Plunged. The pad of the pack slackened, as if

A brooch had been loosened. But when the bull
Returned to the herd, the revolving collar was tighter. And
    only

    The windward owl, uplifted on white wings
        In the glass of air, alert for her young,
    Soared high enough to look into the cleared centre
        And grasp the cause. To the slow brain
Of each beast by the frozen lake what lay in the cradle of their
    crowned

    Heads of horn was a sort of god-head. Its brows
        Nudged when the ark was formed. Its need
    Was a delicate womb away from the iron collar
        Of death, a cave in the ring of horn
Their encircling flesh had backed with fur. That the collar of
    death

    Was the bone of their own skulls: that a softer womb
        Would open between far hills in a plunge
    Of bunched muscles: and that their immortal calf lay
        Dead on the snow with its horns dug into
The ice for grass: they neither saw nor felt. And yet if

    That hill of fur could split and run – like a river
        Of ice in thaw, like a broken grave –
    It would crack across the icy crust of withdrawn
        Sustenance and the rigid circle
Of death be shivered: the fed herd would entail its under-fur

    On the swell of a soft hill and the future be sown
        On grass, I thought. But the herd fell
    By the bank of the lake on the plain, and the pack closed,
        And the ice remained. And I saw that the god
In their ark of horn was a god of love, who made them die.

GEORGE MACBETH

Fantasy of an African Boy

Such a peculiar lot
we are, we people
without money, in daylong
yearlong sunlight, knowing
money is somewhere, somewhere.

Everybody says it's a big
bigger brain bother now,
money. Such millions and millions
of us don't manage at all
without it, like war going on.

And we can't eat it. Yet
without it our heads alone
stay big, as lots and lots do,
coming from nowhere joyful,
going nowhere happy.

We can't drink it up. Yet
without it we shrivel when small
and stop forever
where we stopped,
as lots and lots do.

We can't read money for books.
Yet without it we don't
read, don't write numbers,
don't open gates in other countries,
as lots and lots never do.

We can't use money to bandage
sores, can't pound it
to powder for sick eyes
and sick bellies. Yet without
it, flesh melts from our bones.

Such walled-round gentlemen
overseas minding money! Such
bigtime gentlemen, body guarded
because of too much respect
and too many wishes on them.

Too many wishes everywhere,
wanting them to let go
magic of money, and let it fly
away, everywhere, day and night,
just like dropped leaves in the wind!

JAMES BERRY

The Ballad of the Shrieking Man

A shrieking man stood in the square
And he harangued the smart café
In which a bowlered codger sat
A-twirling of a fine moustache
A-drinking of a fine Tokay

And it was Monday and the town
Was working in a kind of peace
Excepting where the shrieking man
A-waving of his tattered limbs
Glared at the codger's trouser-crease

Saying

Coffee's mad
And tea is mad
And so are gums and teeth and lips.
The horror ships that ply the seas
The horror tongues that plough the teeth
The coat
The tie

The trouser clips
The purple sergeant with the bugger-grips
Will string you up with all their art
And laugh their socks off as you blow apart.

The codger seeming not to hear
Winked at the waiter, paid the bill
And walked the main street out of town
Beyond the school, beyond the works
Where the shrieking man pursued him still
And there the town beneath them lay
And there the desperate river ran.
The codger smiled a purple smile.
A finger sliced his waistcoat ope
And he rounded on the shrieking man

Saying

Tramps are mad
And truth is mad
And so are trees and trunks and tracks.
The horror maps have played us true.
The horror moon that slits the clouds
The gun
The goon
The burlap sacks
The purple waistcoats of the natterjacks
Have done their bit as you can see
To prise the madness from our sanity.

On Wednesday when the day was young
Two shrieking men came into town
And stopped before the smart café
In which another codger sat
Twirling his whiskers with a frown

And as they shrieked and slapped their knees
The codger's toes began to prance

Within the stitching of their caps
Which opened like a set of jaws
And forced him out to join the dance

Saying

Arms are mad
And legs are mad
And all the spaces in between.
The horror spleen that bursts its sack
The horror purple as it lunges through
The lung
The bung
The jumping-bean
The I-think-you-know-what-you-think-I-mean
Are up in arms against the state
And all the body will disintegrate.

On Saturday the town was full
As people strolled in seeming peace
Until three shrieking men appeared
And danced before the smart café
And laughed and jeered and slapped their knees

And there a hundred codgers sat.
A hundred adam's apples rose
And rubbed against their collar studs
Until the music came in thuds
And all the men were on their toes

Saying

Hearts are mad
And minds are mad
And bats are moons and moons are bats.
The horror cats that leap the tiles
The horror slates that catch the wind
The lice
The meat

The burning ghats
The children buried in the butter vats
The steeple crashing through the bedroom roof
Will be your answer if you need a proof.

The codgers poured into the square
And soon their song was on all lips
And all did dance and slap their knees
Until a horseman came in view –
The sergeant with the bugger-grips!

He drew his cutlass, held it high
And brought it down on hand and head
And ears were lopped and limbs were chopped
And still the sergeant slashed and slew
Until the codger crew lay dead

Saying

God is mad
And I am mad
And I am God and you are me.
The horror peace that boils the sight
The horror God turning out the light.
The Christ
Who killed
The medlar tree
Is planning much the same for you and me
And here's a taste of what's in store –
Come back again if you should want some more.

On Sunday as they hosed the streets
I went as usual to pray
And cooled my fingers at the stoup
And when the wafer touched my tongue
I thought about that fine Tokay

And so I crossed the empty square
And met the waiter with a wink

A-sweeping up of severed heads
A-piling up of bowler hats
And he muttered as he poured my drink

Saying

Waiting's mad
And stating's mad
And understating's mad as hell.
The undertakings we have made
The wonder breaking from the sky
The pin
The pen
The poisoned well
The purple sergeant with the nitrate smell
Have won their way and while we wait
The horror ships have passed the straits —
The vice
The vine
The strangler fig
The fault of thinking small and acting big
Have primed the bomb and pulled the pin
And we're all together when the roof falls in!

JAMES FENTON

A Grin

There was this hidden grin.
It wanted a permanent home. It tried faces
In their forgetful moments, the face for instance
Of a woman pushing a baby out between her legs
But that didn't last long the face
Of a man so preoccupied
With the flying steel in the instant
Of the car-crash he left his face

To itself that was even shorter, the face
Of a machine-gunner a long burst not long enough and
The face of a steeplejack the second
Before he hit the paving, the faces
Of two lovers in the seconds
They got so far into each other they forgot
Each other completely that was O.K.
But none of it lasted.

So the grin tried the face
Of somebody lost in sobbing
A murderer's face and the racking moments
Of the man smashing everything
He could reach and had strength to smash
Before he went beyond his body.

It tried the face
In the electric chair to get a tenure
In eternal death, but that too relaxed.
The grin
Sank back, temporarily nonplussed,
Into the skull.

TED HUGHES

Not Like That

It's so pure in the cemetery.
The children love to play up here.
It's a little town, a game of blocks,
a village packed in a box,
a pre-war German toy.
The turf is a bedroom carpet:
heal-all, strawberry flower
and hillocks of moss.
To come and sit here forever,

a cup of tea on one's lap
and one's eyes closed lightly, lightly,
perfectly still
in a nineteenth-century sleep!
it seems so normal to die.

Nobody sleeps here, children.
The little beds of white wrought iron
and the tall, kind, faceless nurse
are somewhere else, in a hospital
or the dreams of prisoners of war.
The drawers of this trunk are empty,
not even a snapshot
curls in a corner.

In Pullmans of childhood we lay
enthralled behind dark-green curtains,
and a little lamp burned blue
all night, for us. The day
was a dream too, even the oatmeal
under its silver lid, dream-cereal
spooned out in forests of spruce
skirting the green-black gorges,
thick woods of sleep, half prickle,
half lakes of fern.
To stay here forever
is not like that, nor even
simply to lie quite still,
the warm trickle of dream
staining the thick quiet.
The drawers of this trunk are empty.
They are all out of sleep up here.

ADRIENNE RICH

A Dream of Hanging

He rang me up
In a dream,
My brother did.
He had been hanged
That morning,
Innocent,
And I had slept
Through the striking
Of the clock
While it had taken place,
Eight,
Just about time enough
For it to happen.
He spoke to me
On the telephone
That afternoon
To reassure me,
My dear brother
Who had killed nobody,
And I asked him,
Long distance,
What it had felt like
To be hanged.
'Oh, don't worry, lovey,' he said,
'When your time comes.
It tickled rather.'

PATRICIA BEER

Defying Gravity

Gravity is one of the oldest tricks in the book.
Let go of the book and it abseils to the ground
As if, at the centre of the earth, spins a giant yo-yo
To which everything is attached by an invisible string.

Tear out a page of the book and make an aeroplane.
Launch it. For an instant it seems that you have fashioned
A shape that can outwit air, that has slipped the knot.
But no. The earth turns, the winch tightens, it is wound in.

One of my closest friends is, at the time of writing,
Attempting to defy gravity, and will surely succeed.
Eighteen months ago he was playing rugby,
Now, seven stones lighter, his wife carries him aw-

Kwardly from room to room. Arranges him gently
Upon the sofa for the visitors. 'How are things?'
Asks one, not wanting to know. Pause. 'Not too bad.'
(Open brackets. Condition inoperable. Close brackets.)

Soon now, the man that I love (not the armful of bones)
Will defy gravity. Freeing himself from the tackle
He will sidestep the opposition and streak down the wing
Towards a dimension as yet unimagined.

Back where the strings are attached there will be a service
And homage paid to the giant yo-yo. A box of left-overs
Will be lowered into a space on loan from the clay.
Then, weighted down, the living will walk wearily away.

ROGER MCGOUGH

Dance of the Cherry Blossom

Both of us are getting worse
Neither knows who had it first

He thinks I gave it to him
I think he gave it to me

Nights chasing clues where
One memory runs into another like dye.

Both of us are getting worse
I know I'm wasting precious time

But who did he meet between
May 87 and March 89.

I feel his breath on my back
A slow climb into himself then out.

In the morning it all seems different
Neither knows who had it first

We eat breakfast together – newspapers
And silence except for the slow slurp of tea

This companionship is better than anything
He thinks I gave it to him.

By lunchtime we're fighting over some petty thing
He tells me I've lost my sense of humour

I tell him I'm not Glaswegian
You all think death is a joke

It's not funny. I'm dying for fuck's sake
I think he gave it to me.

Just think he says it's every couple's dream
I won't have to wait for you up there

I'll have you night after night – your glorious legs
Your strong hard belly, your kissable cheeks

I cry when he says things like that
My shoulders cave in, my breathing trapped

Do you think you have a corner on dying
You self-pitying wretch, pathetic queen.

He pushes me; we roll on the floor like whirlwind;
When we are done in, our lips find each other

We touch soft as breeze, caress the small parts
Rocking back and forth, his arms become mine

There's nothing outside but the noise of the wind
The cherry blossom's dance through the night.

JACKIE KAY

Death & Co.

Two, of course there are two.
It seems perfectly natural now –
The one who never looks up, whose eyes are lidded
And balled, like Blake's,
Who exhibits

The birthmarks that are his trademark –
The scald scar of water,
The nude
Verdigris of the condor.
I am red meat. His beak

Claps sidewise: I am not his yet.
He tells me how badly I photograph.
He tells me how sweet
The babies look in their hospital
Icebox, a simple

Frill at the neck,
Then the flutings of their Ionian
Death-gowns,
Then two little feet.
He does not smile or smoke.

The other does that,
His hair long and plausive.
Bastard
Masturbating a glitter,
He wants to be loved.

I do not stir.
The frost makes a flower,
The dew makes a star,
The dead bell,
The dead bell.

Somebody's done for.

SYLVIA PLATH

Warm to the Cuddly-toy Charm of a Koala Bear

It's dull in the huge palace where I live.
The basement's stuffed with seduced handkerchiefs.
A global war would do, or a new revolution,
To dissipate the gloom of early spring.
Everything's wet – but most the men and women –
Outside, where the long rains drip from the trees.

I'm lonely. There's nobody here but me.
The vintages go round and round in my head,
A merry-go-round I suppose I ought to call it.
Cobwebbed bottles and a thousand dirty glasses,
One in my hand.

Enthusiasm belongs *outside* – and mostly it's bogus.
I live in a mood, with a boozer's conk,
I'm no Prince Charming,
But I'm genuine, genuine, true to my dirty self.

GAVIN EWART

Dream of a Slave

I want to be carried, heavily sedated,
Into a waiting aircraft.
I want to collapse from nervous exhaustion.
I want to bow my head like Samson
And bring down with me
The ten top advertising agencies.

I want to see the little bosses
Vanish in the limelight like harmless fairies.
I want the pantomime to be over,
The circus empty.

I want what is real to establish itself,
My children to prevail,
To live happy ever after
In this world that worships the preposterous.

It is better to be a scribe
Than hacking in the salt-mines,
Heaving the building blocks.
Everybody wants to be a scribe.

But I want out. I want non-existence,
A passive dream, a future for my children.

GAVIN EWART

Song

I chuck my Bible in the parlour fire.
The snake that lives behind the bars there
Sucks at the black book and sweats light;

As they burn together, the codex
Flips its pages over as if reading itself aloud
Memorizing its own contents as it ascends curtseying

Like crowds of grey skirts in the chimney-lift,
In particles of soot like liberated print.
The vacant text glows white on pages that are black.

The stars, those illustrious watchers
Arranged in their picture-codes
With their clear heartbeats and their eager reading stares

Watch the guest ascend. Around us in the parlour
The inn-sign creaks like rowlocks.
The drinkers glower as my book burns,

Their brows look black
Like open books that turning thoughts consume.
Then all at once

With a gesture identical and simultaneous
Of reaching through the coat right into the heart
They all bring out their breast-pocket bibles

Like leather coals and pile them in the fire
And as they burn the men begin to sing
With voices sharp and warm as hearth-flames.

The black pads turn their gilded edges and
The winged stories of the angels rise
And all that remains is our gathering's will

Which assembles into song. Each man sings
Something that he has overheard, or learnt,
Some sing in tongues I do not understand,

But one man does not sing. I notice him
As my song takes me with the others. He is
Setting down the words in rapid shorthand

In a small fat pocketbook with gilded edges.

PETER REDGROVE

Hitcher

I'd been tired, under
the weather, but the ansaphone kept screaming:
One more sick-note, mister, and you're finished. Fired.
I thumbed a lift to where the car was parked.
A Vauxhall Astra. It was hired.

I picked him up in Leeds.
He was following the sun to west from east
with just a toothbrush and the good earth for a bed. The truth,
he said, was blowin' in the wind,
or round the next bend.

I let him have it
on the top road out of Harrogate – once
with the head, then six times with the krooklok
in the face – and didn't even swerve.
I dropped it into third

and leant across
to let him out, and saw him in the mirror
bouncing off the kerb, then disappearing down the verge.
We were the same age, give or take a week.
He'd said he liked the breeze

to run its fingers
through his hair. It was twelve noon.
The outlook for the day was moderate to fair.

Fuck you, I remember thinking,
you can walk from there.

SIMON ARMITAGE

Species

When you look at me as if to say
That's the first meaningful thing you've said in months
I immediately want to take it all back
into a small purse, and let someone else pay.

I want to get drunker than I was last April
and not to be bothered to do all the things I suddenly know
I can do without trying.
I want to hand in my notice.
I want to sit in the kitchen wearing my trusty blue shirt
and read *Parade's End* from page 1 to page 906
without answering the phone, the door or the call of nature.
I want to go back twenty years to a Friday night in the Café
     Amphitryon
and start my life again from there
and be stubborn enough to repeat it all exactly
down to the last visit to the fucking launderette.

I want to stand with you in front of an endangered species –
200 in the president-for-life's reserve, then sixty,
the single final innocent misfit
comatose in its sleeping quarters or scraping its flank
against the bars, a sad disappointment
after the vivid illustrations in the books for children –
and see where that gets us.

CHARLES BOYLE

Dreaming in the Shanghai Restaurant

I would like to be that elderly Chinese gentleman.
He wears a gold watch with a gold bracelet,
But a shirt without sleeves or tie.
He has good luck moles on his face, but is not disfigured with
    fortune.
His wife resembles him, but is still a handsome woman,
She has never bound her feet or her belly.
Some of the party are his children, it seems,
And some his grandchildren;
No generation appears to intimidate another.
He is interested in people, without wanting to convert them or
    pervert them.
He eats with gusto, but not with lust;
And he drinks, but is not drunk.
He is content with his age, which has always suited him.
When he discusses a dish with the pretty waitress,
It is the dish he discusses, not the waitress.
The table-cloth is not so clean as to show indifference,
Not so dirty as to signify a lack of manners.
He proposes to pay the bill but knows he will not be allowed
    to.
He walks to the door like a man who doesn't fret about being
    respected, since he is;
A daughter or granddaughter opens the door for him,
And he thanks her.
It has been a satisfying evening. Tomorrow
Will be a satisfying morning. In between he will sleep
    satisfactorily.
I guess that for him it is peace in his time.
It would be agreeable to be this Chinese gentleman.

D. J. ENRIGHT

A Consumer's Report

The name of the product I tested is *Life*,
I have completed the form you sent me
and understand that my answers are confidential.

I had it as a gift,
I didn't feel much while using it,
in fact I think I'd have liked to be more excited.
It seemed gentle on the hands
but left an embarrassing deposit behind.
It was not economical
and I have used much more than I thought
(I suppose I have about half left
but it's difficult to tell) –
although the instructions are fairly large
there are so many of them
I don't know which to follow, especially
as they seem to contradict each other.
I'm not sure such a thing
should be put in the way of children –
It's difficult to think of a purpose
for it. One of my friends says
it's just to keep its maker in a job.
Also the price is much too high.
Things are piling up so fast,
after all, the world got by
for a thousand million years
without this, do we need it now?
(Incidentally, please ask your man
to stop calling me 'the respondent',
I don't like the sound of it.)
There seems to be a lot of different labels,
sizes and colours should be uniform,
the shape is awkward, it's waterproof
but not heat resistant, it doesn't keep

yet it's very difficult to get rid of:
whenever they make it cheaper they seem
to put less in – if you say you don't
want it, then it's delivered anyway.
I'd agree it's a popular product,
it's got into the language; people
even say they're on the side of it.
Personally I think it's overdone,
a small thing people are ready
to behave badly about. I think
we should take it for granted. If its
experts are called philosophers or market
researchers or historians, we shouldn't
care. We are the consumers and the last
law makers. So finally, I'd buy it.
But the question of a 'best buy'
I'd like to leave until I get
the competitive product you said you'd send.

PETER PORTER

When a Beautiful Woman Gets on the Jutiapa Bus

babies twist in their mothers' arms. The men
yearn so the breath snags, Ai! in their chests.
The women flick their eyes over her,
discreet, and turn back to each other.

                          When
a beautiful woman steps on the bus, she scowls
with the arrogance of the gorgeous. That face,
engrave it on commemorative stamps. A philatelist's
dream. That profile should be stamped on centennial
coins. Somebody quick take a picture of her,
la señora in the azure frock. Sculpt her image
to honor Our Lady.

Just how did she land here,
Miss Fine Mix? As a matter of course, her forefather,
El Conquistador, raped a Mayan priestess,
Anno Domini 1510. At the moment of her own conception,
her parents met each other's eyes. Don't stare.

What's she doing squeezed in here with campesinos
carrying chickens? Squawk. Save that face.

When a beautiful woman gets off the bus, everyone
sighs, Ai! and imagines her fate: she's off
to Sunday dinner with mama who's groomed her
to marry an honest farmer happy to knock her up
every spring. Her looks (no doubt) will leach out,
washing the dead, schlepping headloads of scavenged
firewood, grinding, grinding, grinding corn,
hanging the wash in the sun and wind, all
by hand, all by her graceful brown hand.

BELLE WARING

Being a Wife

So this is what it's like being a wife.
The body I remember feeling as big as America in,
the thighs so far away
his hand had to ride in an aeroplane to get there;
the giggles I heard adults giggling with
I was puzzled about,
and felt much too solemn to try;
buttons unbuttoned by somebody else, not me;
the record-player
neither of us were able to stop what we were doing
to turn off;
the smell of fish
I dreaded I'd never get used to,

the peculiar, leering, antediluvian taste
I preferred not to taste;
the feeling of being on the edge of something
everyone older than us,
had wasted,
and not understood,
as we were about to do;
his pink hand gripping my breast
as if his life depended on it;
the shame of the thought of the mirror
reflecting all this,
seem long ago,
yet somehow authentic and right.
Being a wife is like acting being a wife,
and the me that was her with him in the past is still me.

SELIMA HILL

Against Coupling

I write in praise of the solitary act:
of not feeling a trespassing tongue
forced into one's mouth, one's breath
smothered, nipples crushed against the
ribcage, and that metallic tingling
in the chin set off by a certain odd nerve:

unpleasure. Just to avoid those eyes would help –
such eyes as a young girl draws life from,
listening to the vegetal
rustle within her, as his gaze
stirs polypal fronds in the obscure
sea-bed of her body, and her own eyes blur.

There is much to be said for abandoning
this no longer novel exercise –
for not 'participating in

a total experience' – when
one feels like the lady in Leeds who
had seen *The Sound of Music* eighty-six times;

or more, perhaps, like the school drama mistress
producing *A Midsummer Night's Dream*
for the seventh year running, with
yet another cast from 5B.
Pyramus and Thisbe are dead, but
the hole in the wall can still be troublesome.

I advise you, then, to embrace it without
encumbrance. No need to set the scene,
dress up (or undress), make speeches.
Five minutes of solitude are
enough – in the bath, or to fill
that gap between the Sunday papers and lunch.

FLEUR ADCOCK

The Ecstasy of St Saviour's Avenue

(*Valentine's Night*)

Tonight the tenement smells of oysters
and semen, chocolate and rose petals.
The windows of every flat are open
to cool us, the noise of our limberings
issues from every sash as if the building
was hyperventilating in the cold
February air. We can hear the moans
of the Rossiters, the Hendersons,
the babysitters in number 3; a gentle
pornography rousing us like an aphrodisiac.
For once the house is harmonious, we rock
in our beds; our rhythms hum
in the stone foundations.

We shall have to be careful;
like soldiers who must break step on a bridge.
We stagger our climaxes one by one,
from the basement flat to the attic room,
a pounding of mattresses moves through the house
in a long, multiple, communal orgasm.
The building sighs like a whorehouse.
We lie in our sheets watching the glow
of the street lights colour the sky; the chimneys
blow their smoke like the mellow exhalations
of post-coital cigarettes.

NEIL ROLLINSON

The Sheep Child

Farm boys wild to couple
With anything   with soft-wooded trees
With mounds of earth   mounds
Of pinestraw   will keep themselves off
Animals by legends of their own:
In the hay-tunnel dark
And dung of barns, they will
Say   I have heard tell

That in a museum in Atlanta
Way back in a corner somewhere
There's this thing that's only half
Sheep   like a woolly baby
Pickled in alcohol   because
Those things can't live   his eyes
Are open   but you can't stand to look
I heard from somebody who...

But this is now almost all
Gone. The boys have taken

Their own true wives in the city,
The sheep are safe in the west hill
Pasture   but we who were born there
Still are not sure. Are we,
Because we remember, remembered
In the terrible dust of museums?

Merely with his eyes, the sheep-child may

Be saying   saying

I am here, in my father's house.
I who am half of your world, came deeply
To my mother in the long grass
Of the west pasture, where she stood like moonlight
Listening for foxes. It was something like love
From another world that seized her
From behind, and she gave, not lifting her head
Out of dew, without ever looking, her best
Self to that great need. Turned loose, she dipped her face
Farther into the chill of the earth, and in a sound
Of sobbing   of something stumbling
Away, began as she must do,
To carry me. I woke, dying,

In the summer sun of the hillside, with my eyes
Far more than human. I saw for a blazing moment
The great grassy world from both sides,
Man and beast in the round of their need,
And the hill wind stirred in my wool,
My hoof and my hand clasped each other,
I ate my one meal
Of milk, and died
Staring. From dark grass I came straight

To my father's house, whose dust
Whirls up in the halls for no reason
When no one comes   piling deep in a hellish mild corner,

And, through my immortal waters,
I meet the sun's grains eye
To eye, and they fail at my closet of glass.
Dead, I am most surely living
In the minds of farm boys: I am he who drives
Them like wolves from the hound bitch and calf
And from the chaste ewe in the wind.
They go into woods   into bean fields   they go
Deep into their known right hands. Dreaming of me,
They groan   they wait   they suffer
Themselves, they marry, they raise their kind.

JAMES DICKEY

The Geranium

When I put her out, once, by the garbage pail,
She looked so limp and bedraggled,
So foolish and trusting, like a sick poodle,
Or a wizened aster in late September,
I brought her back in again
For a new routine—
Vitamins, water, and whatever
Sustenance seemed sensible
At the time: she'd lived
So long on gin, bobbie pins, half-smoked cigars, dead beer,
Her shriveled petals falling
On the faded carpet, the stale
Steak grease stuck to her fuzzy leaves.
(Dried-out, she creaked like a tulip.)

The things she endured!—
The dumb dames shrieking half the night
Or the two of us, alone, both seedy,
Me breathing booze at her,
She leaning out of her pot toward the window.

Near the end, she seemed almost to hear me—
And that was scary—
So when that snuffling cretin of a maid
Threw her, pot and all, into the trash-can,
I said nothing.

But I sacked the presumptuous hag the next week,
I was that lonely.

THEODORE ROETHKE

Grimalkin

One of these days she will lie there and be dead.
I'll take her out back in the garbage bag
and bury her among my sons' canaries,
the ill-fated turtles, a pair of angelfish:
the tragic and mannerly household pests
that had the better sense to take their leaves
before their welcomes or my patience had worn thin.
For twelve long years I've suffered this damned cat
while Mike, my darling middle-son, himself
twelve years this coming May, has grown into
the tender if quick-tempered manchild
his breeding blessed and cursed him to become.
And only his affection keeps this cat alive
though more than once I've threatened violence—
the brick and burlap in the river recompense
for mounds of furballs littering the house,
choking the vacuum cleaner, or what's worse:
shit in the closets, piss in the planters, mice
that winter indoors safely as she sleeps
curled about a table-leg, vigilant
as any knick-knack in a partial coma.
But Mike, of course, is blind to all of it—
the grey angora breed of arrogance,

the sluttish roar, the way she disappears for days
sex-desperate once or twice a year,
urgently ripping her way out the screen door
to have her way with anything that moves
while Mike sits up with tuna fish and worry,
crying into the darkness 'here kitty kitty',
mindless of her whorish treacheries
and or of her crimes against upholsteries—
the sofas, love seats, wingbacks, easychairs
she's puked and mauled into dilapidation.
I have this reoccurring dream of driving her
deep into the desert east of town
and dumping her out there with a few days feed
and water. In the dream, she's always found
by kindly tribespeople who eat her kind
on certain holy days as a form of penance.
God knows, I don't know what he sees in her.
Sometimes he holds her like a child in his arms
rubbing her underside until she sounds
like one of those battery powered vibrators
folks claim to use for the ache in their shoulders.
And under Mike's protection she will fix her
indolent green-eyed gaze on me as if
to say: Whaddaya gonna do about it, Slick,
the child loves me and you love the child.
Truth told, I really ought to have her fixed
in the old way with an air-tight alibi,
a bag of ready-mix and no eyewitnesses.
But one of these days she will lie there and be dead.
And choking back loud hallelujahs, I'll pretend
a brief bereavement for my Michael's sake,
letting him think as he has often said
'deep down inside you really love her don't you Dad.'
I'll even hold some cheerful obsequies
careful to observe God's never-failing care
for even these, the least of His creatures,

making some mention of a cat-heaven where
cat-ashes to ashes, cat-dust to dust
and the Lord gives and the Lord has taken away.
Thus claiming my innocence to the bitter end,
I'll turn Mike homeward from that wicked little grave
and if he asks, we'll get another one because
all boys need practice in the arts of love
and all boys' ageing fathers in the arts of rage.

THOMAS LYNCH

Before You Cut Loose,

                  put dogs on the list
of difficult things to lose. Those dogs ditched
on the North York Moors or the Sussex Downs
or hurled like bags of sand from rented cars
have followed their noses to market towns
and bounced like balls into their owners' arms.
I heard one story of a dog that swam
to the English coast from the Isle of Man,
and a dog that carried eggs and bacon
and a morning paper from the village
surfaced umpteen leagues and two years later,
bacon eaten but the eggs unbroken,
newsprint dry as tinder, to the letter.
A dog might wander the width of the map
to bury its head in its owner's lap,
crawl the last mile to dab a bleeding paw
against its own front door. To die at home,
a dog might walk its four legs to the bone.
You can take off the tag and the collar
but a dog wears one coat and one colour.
A dog got rid of – that's a dog for life.

No dog howls like a dog kicked out at night.
Try looking a dog like that in the eye.

SIMON ARMITAGE

The Strange Case

My dog's assumed my alter ego.
Has taken over – walks the house
phallus hanging wealthy and raw
in front of guests, nuzzling
head up skirts
while I direct my mandarin mood.

Last week driving the baby sitter home.
She, unaware dog sat in the dark back seat,
talked on about the kids' behaviour.
On Huron Street the dog leaned forward
and licked her ear.
The car going 40 miles an hour
she seemed more amazed
at my driving ability
than my indiscretion.

It was only the dog I said.
Oh she said.
Me interpreting her reply all the way home.

MICHAEL ONDAATJE

Country Fair

for Hayden Carruth

If you didn't see the six-legged dog,
It doesn't matter.
We did and he mostly lay in the corner.
As for the extra legs,

One got used to them quickly
And thought of other things.
Like, what a cold, dark night
To be out at the fair.

Then the keeper threw a stick
And the dog went after it
On four legs, the other two flapping behind,
Which made one girl shriek with laughter.

She was drunk and so was the man
Who kept kissing her neck.
The dog got the stick and looked back at us.
And that was the whole show.

CHARLES SIMIC

Dancing in Vacationland

for Kevin Boyle

The people in the houses behind Searsport are dancing:
the people in tin and tar paper mobile homes, people
in plywood shacks surrounded by junked cars and tires,
broken furniture, hungry geese and chickens, bored
hunting dogs. In ones and twos, they open their doors,
weaving and bobbing out to the road: men in gray
work clothes, women in baggy print dresses; the people
who process chickens, stick fingers down chicken throats

as the chickens come dangling down the line, tearing
out windpipes, tearing out guts; the men and women
who pick meat out of crab bodies, arrange sardines
in little cans; men who work the docks in all weather,
who try to run lobster boats throughout the winter.
These people are now dancing from their houses of
wreckage where they scream at each other and raise
ignorant children and hang on to each other at night.
In threes and fours, they dance toward Searsport and
Route 1. Then, reaching town, they form a single line,
dancing with their arms on their neighbors' shoulders,
dancing in one long row between the shiny antique shops
and fat realtors: one foot up, one foot down, step
to the right, step to the left – lining the highway
which is crowded with tourists from the south
trying to soak up picturesque views of the ocean.
But this morning all they can see are people dancing,
these bloated potato-fed people dancing, these people
who live by collecting returnable bottles, by picking
over the trash at the dump, by trading their bodies,
their wits, their health for a few dollars
and a shack behind Searsport. This morning, because
it is warm and sunny and because they just can't
stand it anymore, they decided to start dancing:
one foot up, one foot down. And the tourists from New York
stop their cars and the tourists from Massachusetts
take pictures and the tourists from Connecticut
feed candy to the little ones, until at last the realtors
and tour guide directors and lobster shack owners,
until at last the alternative life-style farmers,
gift-shop operators, local chamber of commerce,
town police, state police and sheriff's department
all band together and a spokesperson apologizes
to the tourists from the south and begs them
to take no more pictures; and they try to make
the people stop dancing, but the people won't listen

and keep right on dancing – one foot up, one foot down –
so they push them back off Route 1, push them back
to the little roads behind Searsport, push them back
into the tin and tar paper mobile homes, the plywood
shacks surrounded by junked cars, but through the windows
they can still be seen dancing, dancing into the night
in their little paper houses, until at last they lie down
and hold on to each other, hang on to each other
as if afraid of sinking into the earth, afraid the whole
vacationland world might stop spinning beneath them.

STEPHEN DOBYNS

1668

In 1667 a small party of British marines was landed on the
islands of Bombay, to take possession of them. The islands
formed part of the dowry brought by the Portuguese princess,
Catherine de Braganza, to Charles II, the English king.

The flux dehydrates my flesh. Common
Enough, the apothecary tells me,
On these islands, in this weather.
But he proffers no sound remedy,
Though the swamps breed so many leeches
As would bleed half London for a day.
The churches and taverns are seas away.
We are wet scarecrows, sleepy keepers
Of beslimed acres, ourselves beslimed.
Great fish leap in the beached nets.
We eat fish; our liquor tastes of fish.
The orifices of the black fishwives
Smell of too much fish, like to my stool
Which I, bowed under rain, bury
On this beach where each man is changed:
Dowry for a dupe, corpses' ransom,

Fiction of the brindled Portuguese
Whose Christ, marooned in the marshland,
Held a wry hand up in benediction.
Estuary water and the mangrove trellis
Wrapped and obscured Him, left only
The lifted hand to bless unmapped waves,
Our graves also, if no sail come.
Our names listed in no parish, no deed
That we, forsaken, before our undoing did
More than a hand raised from water as token.
So are we broken, so obliterated...

DOM MORAES

Austerities

From the heel
Of a half loaf
Of black bread,
They made a child's head.

Child, they said,
We've nothing for eyes,
Nothing to spare for ears
And nose.

Just a knife
To make a slit
Where your mouth
Ought to be.

You can grin,
You can eat,
Spit the crumbs
Into our faces.

CHARLES SIMIC

Nigger Sweat

'Please have your passport and all documents out and ready for your interview. Kindly keep them dry.' Notice in Waiting-room, U.S. Embassy, Visa Section, Kingston, 1983

No disrespect, mi boss,
just honest nigger sweat;
well almost, for is true
some of we trying to fool you
so we can lose weself
on the Big R ranch
to find a little life;
but, boss, is hard times
make it, and not because
black people born wutliss:
so, boss, excuse this nigger sweat.
And I know that you know it
as well as me,
this river running through history
this historical fact, this sweat
that put the aroma
in your choice Virginia
that sweeten the cane
and make the cotton shine;
and sometimes I dream a nightmare dream
that the river rising, rising
and swelling the sea and I see
you choking and drowning
in a sea of black man sweat
and I wake up shaking
with shame and remorse
for my mother did teach me,
Child, don't study revenge.
Don't think we not grateful, boss,
how you cool down the place for we comfort,
but the line shuffle forward

one step at a time
like Big Fraid hold we,
and the cool-cut, crew-cut Marine boy
wid him ice-blue eye and him walkie-talkie
dissa walk through the place and pretend
him no see we.
But a bring me handkerchief,
mi mother did bring me up right,
and, God willing, I keeping things cool
till we meet face to face,
and a promise you, boss,
if I get through I gone,
gone from this bruk-spirit, kiss-me-arse place.

EDWARD BAUGH

The Emigrant Irish

Like oil lamps we put them out the back,

of our houses, of our minds. We had lights
better than, newer than and then

a time came, this time and now
we need them. Their dread, makeshift example.

They would have thrived on our necessities.
What they survived we could not even live.
By their lights now it is time to
imagine how they stood there, what they stood with,
that their possessions may become our power.

Cardboard. Iron. Their hardships parcelled in them.
Patience. Fortitude. Long-suffering
in the bruise-coloured dusk of the New World.

And all the old songs. And nothing to lose.

EAVAN BOLAND

The Woman on the Dump

Where was it one first heard the truth? The the.
WALLACE STEVENS

She sits on a smoldering couch
reading labels from old tin cans,
the ground ground down
to dirt, hard as poured cement.
A crowd of fat white gulls
take mincing, oblique steps
around the couch, searching for
an orange rind, a crab claw.
Clouds scud backward overhead,
drop quickly over the horizon,
as if weighted with lead sinkers.
The inside's outside here,
her 'sitting room' *en plein air:*
a homey triad of chaise longue,
tilting table, and old floor lamp
from a torn-down whorehouse,
the shade a painted scene
of nymphs in a naked landscape.
The lamp is a beautiful thing,
even if she can't plug it in,
the bare-cheeked, breathless
nymphs part of the eternal
feminine as they rush away
from streaming trees and clouds
that can't be trusted not to change
from man to myth and back again.
The dump's too real. Or not
real enough. It is hot here.
Or cold. When the sun goes down,
she wraps herself in old newspaper,
the newsprint rubbing off,

so that she *is* the news as she
looks for clues and scraps
of things in the refuse. The *the*
is here somewhere, buried
under bulldozed piles of trash.
She picks up a pair of old cymbals
to announce the moon, the pure
symbol, just coming up over there.
Abandoned bathtubs, sinks, and stoves
glow white – abstract forms
in the moonlight – a high tide
of garbage spawns and grows,
throwing long lovely shadows
across unplumbed ravines and gullies.
She'll work through the night,
the woman on the dump,
sifting and sorting and putting
things right, saving everything
that can be saved, rejecting
nothing, piles of tires
in the background unexhaustedly
burning, burning, burning.

ELIZABETH SPIRES

The Man Who Invented Pain

He lifted the wicker lid
and pigeons poured
past his hands,

a ravel of light
like oxygen
escaping underwater.

Loss of privileges
in peacetime; in war,
a capital offence.

He offered no defence,
simply composed
a non-existent life

in letters home,
enough for a year,
to be posted in order,

of which the last began:
Dear Mother, Dear Dad,
Thanks for yours.

Today, a Tuesday,
we shot a man
at 0800 hours.

Try to imagine,
if you can,
the subdued feel

of a Sunday morning
and the quiet clash
of a dixie lid,

lifting and lapsing
like a censer
at mass.

Imagine held hats,
blown about hair
and the firing squad

down on one knee,
close enough to see
his Adam's apple

genuflect
just once
before they fired.

And then imagine
the rest of the day:
the decent interval

before the men
began to form a queue
with mess tins,

the way in which
the day remained
a Sunday until dark.

Things were touched
with reverence.
Even the sergeant,

feeling for fags
in his battle dress,
patted his pockets

uncertainly,
in turn, and again,
as if he'd forgotten

the sign of the cross,
and the captain
on a canvas stool

sat like a priest,
with praying eyes
and inclined head,

while his batman cut
and curls fell
all over his surplice.

Imagine the sun
waking the flies
to a confessional buzz

in the camp latrines,
and each latrine
a taut box kite

waiting for wind
on the kind of day
a man might read

the Sunday paper
by his pigeon cree,
or nervously

walk out to bat
and notice the green
on a fielder's knee.

CRAIG RAINE

'now is a ship'

now is a ship

which captain am
sails out of sleep

steering for dream

E. E. CUMMINGS

The Italians Are Excited

The Italians are excited.
They keep standing up to look out of the train.
Spring sunshine ripens their hands and accents,

Spring sunshine colours winter trees and rubbish.
They cannot be admiring the landscape, yet one would think
They were just entering the Ticino and passing the first
    vineyard.
They keep standing up to look over the head of the driver.
They must be gauging the advancing complexity of rails
Or the Englishness of English overhead wiring.
They are not interested in the driver
Or the sun yellowing their hands.

Only when the train nears the city station
Do they empty their eyes and sit down in silence.

FREDA DOWNIE

The Railway Station

i: *the indicator*

a wooden saint
in need of paint

the indicator
has turned inward
ten times over

swallowed the names
of all the railway
stations it knows

removed its hands
from its face
and put them away
in its pockets

if it knows when
the next train's due
it gives no clue

the clockface adds
its numerals

the total is zero

2: *the station dog*

the spirit of the place
lives inside the mangy body
of the station dog

doing penance for the last
three hundred years under
the tree of arrivals and departures

the dog opens his right eye
just long enough to look at you and see
whether you're a man a demon a demigod

or the eight armed railway timetable come
to stroke him on the head
with a healing hand

and to take him to heaven
the dog decides
that day is not yet

3: *the tea stall*

the young novice at the tea stall
has taken a vow of silence

when you ask him a question
he exorcises you

by sprinkling dishwater in your face
and continues with his ablutions in the sink

and certain ceremonies connected
with the washing of cups and saucers

4: *the station master*

the booking clerk believes in the doctrine
of the next train
when conversation turns to time
he takes his tongue
hands it to you across the counter
and directs you to a superior
intelligence

the two headed station master
belongs to a sect
that rejects every timetable
not published in the year the track was laid
as apocryphal
but interprets the first timetable
with a freedom that allows him to read
every subsequent timetable between
the lines of its text

he keeps looking anxiously at the setting sun
as if the sunset were a part of a secret ritual
and he didn't want anything to go wrong with it
at the last minute
finally he nods like a stroke
between a yes and a no
and says
all timetables ever published
along with all timetables yet to be published
are simultaneously valid
at any given time and on any given track
insofar as all the timetables were inherent
in the one printed
when the track was laid

and goes red
in both his faces
at once

5: *vows*

slaughter a goat before the clock
smash a coconut on the railway track
smear the indicator with the blood of a cock
bathe the station master in milk
and promise you will give
a solid gold toy train to the booking clerk
if only someone would tell you
when the next train is due

6: *the setting sun*

the setting sun
touches upon the horizon
at a point where the rails
like the parallels
of a prophecy
appear to meet

the setting sun
large as a wheel

ARUN KOLATKAR

Sleeping Compartment

I don't like this, being carried sideways
through the night. I feel wrong and helpless – like
a timber broadside in a fast stream.

Such a way of moving may suit
that odd snake the sidewinder
in Arizona: but not me in Perthshire.

I feel at rightangles to everything,
a crossgrain in existence. – It scrapes
the top of my head and my footsoles.

To forget outside is no help either –
then I become a blockage
in the long gut of the train.

I try to think I'm an Alice in Wonderland
mountaineer bivouacked
on a ledge five feet high.

It's no good. I go sidelong.
I rock sideways ... I draw in my feet
to let Aviemore pass.

NORMAN MACCAIG

The Taxis

In the first taxi he was alone tra-la,
No extras on the clock. He tipped ninepence
But the cabby, while he thanked him, looked askance
As though to suggest someone had bummed a ride.

In the second taxi he was alone tra-la
But the clock showed sixpence extra; he tipped according
And the cabby from out his muffler said: 'Make sure
You have left nothing behind tra-la between you.'

In the third taxi he was alone tra-la
But the tip-up seats were down and there was an extra
Charge of one-and-sixpence and an odd
Scent that reminded him of a trip to Cannes.

As for the fourth taxi, he was alone
Tra-la when he hailed it but the cabby looked
Through him and said: 'I can't tra-la well take
So many people, not to speak of the dog.'

LOUIS MACNEICE

A Sign Illuminated

In honour of something or other – poor
King Bertie's crowning; the Charter Centenary;
1938 as a whole – the city

decreed that on several occasions there should emerge
from the Depot on Kyotts Lake Road an Illuminated
Bus. On a published route

it would slowly glide through every
suburb and slum in turn. Crowds
might turn out. So it came

cruising on summer evenings, before
the little boys went to their beds, its lights
plain in the sun from as much as a mile off;

those lights were its headlamps and certain thin
patterns of domestic bulbs
all over the coachwork. What the city had picked

was one of its own
retired double-deckers. They'd sliced off the top,
blacked the windows, painted out the livery;

it was a vehicle so old
that the shadowy driver sat exposed above the engine
in an open cab. Among the little boys

were many who knew the design and the period
registration plates. In the sunset light
they could take it all in: this emblem

that trundled past all the stops; possessed no
route number, passengers or conductor; was less
than a bus, let alone less than lit up.

ROY FISHER

Death of a Farmyard

Worn out were the buildings, I
Tell you. Worn out. Do you know how
Buildings wear out? Elm walls were
Worm-bored and warped. Rain

Through the gap. Hard stemmed
Wide weeds in the track. Door hinges
Rusted, dropped out. In the lew, strapped
War-wounded Jim wove ropes out of

Hay. Smell of old hay. High
Nettles. Elders. Staddles, no, did
Not keep out rats. String-
Tailed quick feet, rats nipped

Into sacks. And believe it or not,
Two geese were dead and were dry,
Sitting down white around hollow,
Alongside low sties collapsed.

Pulled away, I tell you, all
Pulled away. No yard, no broken
Hay. No Jim. A new house. A new day.
That muck. All pulled away.

GEOFFREY GRIGSON

The Explosion

On the day of the explosion
Shadows pointed towards the pithead:
In the sun the slagheap slept.

Down the lane came men in pitboots
Coughing oath-edged talk and pipe-smoke,
Shouldering off the freshened silence.

One chased after rabbits; lost them;
Came back with a nest of lark's eggs;
Showed them; lodged them in the grasses.

So they passed in beards and moleskins,
Fathers, brothers, nicknames, laughter,
Through the tall gates standing open.

At noon, there came a tremor; cows
Stopped chewing for a second; sun,
Scarfed as in a heat-haze, dimmed.

The dead go on before us, they
Are sitting in God's house in comfort,
We shall see them face to face—

Plain as lettering in the chapels
It was said, and for a second
Wives saw men of the explosion

Larger than in life they managed—
Gold as on a coin, or walking
Somehow from the sun towards them,

One showing the eggs unbroken.

PHILIP LARKIN

Timer

Gold survives the fire that's hot enough
to make you ashes in a standard urn.
An envelope of coarse official buff
contains your wedding ring which wouldn't burn.

Dad told me I'd to tell them at St James's
that the ring should go in the incinerator.
That 'eternity' inscribed with both their names is
his surety that they'd be together, 'later'.

I signed for the parcelled clothing as the son,
the cardy, apron, pants, bra, dress—

the clerk phoned down: *6–8–8–3–1?*
Has she still her ring on? (Slight pause) *Yes!*

It's on my warm palm now, your burnished ring!

I feel your ashes, head, arms, breasts, womb, legs,
sift through its circle slowly, like that thing
you used to let me watch to time the eggs.

TONY HARRISON

The Scissors Ceremony

What they are doing makes their garden feel like a big room.
I spy on them through the hedge, through a hundred keyholes.
He sits in a deckchair. She leans over him from behind
As though he were a little boy, and clips his fingernails
Into the newspaper he balances between his knees. Her
White hair tickles his white hair. Her breath at his ear
Might be correcting his sums, disclosing the facts of life,
Recalling the other warm cheeks that have hesitated there.
He is not demented or lazy or incapacitated. No,
It is just that she enjoys clipping his fingernails
And scattering them like seeds out of a rattly packet.
Are they growing younger as I walk the length of the hedge?
Look! The scissors ceremony is a way of making love!

MICHAEL LONGLEY

The Plain Sense of Things

After the leaves have fallen, we return
To a plain sense of things. It is as if
We had come to an end of the imagination,
Inanimate in an inert savoir.

It is difficult even to choose the adjective
For this blank cold, this sadness without cause.
The great structure has become a minor house.
No turban walks across the lessened floors.

The greenhouse never so badly needed paint.
The chimney is fifty years old and slants to one side.
A fantastic effort has failed, a repetition
In a repetitiousness of men and flies.

Yet the absence of the imagination had
Itself to be imagined. The great pond,
The plain sense of it, without reflections, leaves,
Mud, water like dirty glass, expressing silence

Of a sort, silence of a rat come out to see,
The great pond and its waste of the lilies, all this
Had to be imagined as an inevitable knowledge,
Required, as a necessity requires.

WALLACE STEVENS

Where Are the Waters of Childhood?

See where the windows are boarded up,
where the gray siding shines in the sun and salt air
and the asphalt shingles on the roof have peeled or fallen off,
where tiers of oxeye daisies float on a sea of grass?
That's the place to begin.

Enter the kingdom of rot,
smell the damp plaster, step over the shattered glass,
the pockets of dust, the rags, the soiled remains of a mattress,
look at the rusted stove and sink, at the rectangular stain
on the wall where Winslow Homer's *Gulf Stream* hung.

Go to the room where your father and mother
would let themselves go in the drift and pitch of love,
and hear, if you can, the creak of their bed,
then go to the place where you hid.

Go to your room, to all the rooms whose cold, damp air you
      breathed,
to all the unwanted places where summer, fall, winter, spring,
seem the same unwanted season, where the trees you knew
      have died
and other trees have risen. Visit that other place
you barely recall, that other house half hidden.

See the two dogs burst into sight. When you leave,
they will cease, snuffed out in the glare of an earlier light.
Visit the neighbors down the block; he waters his lawn,
she sits on her porch, but not for long.
When you look again they are gone.

Keep going back, back to the field, flat and sealed in mist.
On the other side, a man and a woman are waiting;
they have come back, your mother before she was gray,
your father before he was white.

Now look at the North West Arm, how it glows a deep
      cerulean blue.
See the light on the grass, the one leaf burning, the cloud
that flares. You're almost there, in a moment your parents
will disappear, leaving you under the light of a vanished star,
under the dark of a star newly born. Now is the time.

Now you invent the boat of your flesh and set it upon the
   waters
and drift in the gradual swell, in the laboring salt.
Now you look down. The waters of childhood are there.

MARK STRAND

My Mother's Lips

Until I asked her to please stop doing it and was astonished to
   find that she not only could
but from the moment I asked her in fact would stop doing it, my
   mother, all through my childhood,
when I was saying something to her, something important, would
   move her lips as I was speaking
so that she seemed to be saying under her breath the very words I
   was saying as I was saying them.

Or, even more disconcertingly – wildly so now that my puberty
   had erupted – *before* I said them.
When I was smaller, I must just have assumed that she was
   omniscient. Why not?
She knew everything else – when I was tired, or lying; she'd
   know I was ill before I did.
I may even have thought – how could it not have come into my
   mind? – that she *caused* what I said.

All she was really doing of course was mouthing my words a
   split second after I said them myself,
but it wasn't until my own children were learning to talk that I
   really understood how,
and understood, too, the edge of anxiety in it, the wanting to
   bring you along out of the silence,
the compulsion to lift you again from those blank caverns of
   namelessness we encase.

That was long afterward, though: where I was now was just
    wanting to get her to stop,
and, considering how I brooded and raged in those days, how
    quickly my teeth went on edge,
the restraint I approached her with seems remarkable, although
    her so unprotestingly,
readily taming a habit by then three children and a dozen years
    old was as much so.

It's endearing to watch us again in that long-ago dusk, facing
    each other, my mother and me.
I've just grown to her height, or just past it: there are our lips
    moving together,
now the unison suddenly breaks, I have to go on by myself, no
    maestro, no score to follow.
I wonder what finally made me take umbrage enough, or heart
    enough, to confront her?

It's not important. My cocoon at that age was already unwind-
    ing: the threads ravel and snarl.
When I find one again, it's that two o'clock in the morning, a
    grim hotel on a square,
the impenetrable maze of an endless city, when, really alone for
    the first time in my life,
I found myself leaning from the window, incanting in a tearing
    whisper what I thought were poems.

I'd love to know what I raved that night to the night, what those
    innocent dithyrambs were,
or to feel what so ecstatically drew me out of myself and beyond
    ... Nothing is there, though,
only the solemn piazza beneath me, the riot of dim, tiled roofs
    and impassable alleys,
my desolate bed behind me, and my voice, hoarse, and the sweet,
    alien air against me like a kiss.

C. K. WILLIAMS

Calvin Klein's *Obsession*

I raised my glass, and – solid, pungent, like the soot-encrusted
    brickwork
Of the Ulster Brewery – a smell of yeast and hops and malt swam
    up:
I sniff and sniff again, and try to think of what it is I am
    remembering:
I think that's how it goes, like Andy Warhol's calendar of
    perfumes,
Dribs and drabs left over to remind him of that season's smell.
Very personal, of course, as *Blue Grass* is for me the texture of a
    fur
Worn by this certain girl I haven't seen in years. Every time that
    Blue Grass
Hits me, it is 1968. I'm walking with her through the smoggy
    early dusk
Of West Belfast: coal-smoke, hops, fur, the smell of stout and
    whiskey
Breathing out from somewhere. So it all comes back, or nearly
    all.
A long-forgotten kiss.

Never quite. Horses' dung is smoking on the cobbles. Cobble-
    stones?
I must have gone back further than I thought, to brewers' drays
    and milk-carts.
Brylcreem, *Phoenix* beer. Or candy apples – rich hard dark-
    brown glaze
Impossible to bite at first, until you licked and licked and sucked
    a way
Into the soft core. A dark interior, where I'd also buy a twist of
    snuff
For my grandma. She'd put two pinches on a freckled fist, and
    sniff.

Then a sip of whiskey, and, as always, *I'm not long for this world*.

My father would make a face: *a whingeing gate*, he'd say, *hangs longest* –

Hoping it was true, perhaps – a phrase he'd said so often, he'd forgotten

When he said it last. That *Gold Label* whiskey – nearly like a perfume:

I go crazy because I want to smell them all so much,

Warhol's high-pitched New York whine comes on again, with

All those exhalations of the 'thirties and the 'forties: Guerlain's

Sous le Vent, Saravel's *White Christmas*, Corday's *Voyage à Paris*, or

Kathleen Mary Quinlan's *Rhythm*: bottles of bottle-green, bruise-blues

Darker than the pansies at the cemetery gate-lodge, bottles of frosted glass

And palest lilac – *l'odeur de ton sein chaleureux* – a rush of musk

And incense, camphor, beckons from the back of the wardrobe; I'd slipped

Through the mirror in a dream. *Opium* by Yves St Laurent? More than likely,

What my mother used to call a guilty conscience, or something that I ate:

Cheese and chopped dill pickle on wheaten farls, looking, if I thought of it,

Like Boots' *Buttermilk and Clover* soap –

Slipping and slipping from my grasp, clunking softly downwards through

The greying water; I have drowsed off into something else. The ornate fish

And frog and water-lily motif on the bathroom wallpaper reminds me

How in fact I'd stripped it off some months ago. It was April, a
     time
Of fits and starts; fresh leaves blustered at the window, strips
     and fronds
Of fish and water-lilies sloughed off round my feet. A Frank
     Ifield song
From 1963, I think, kept coming back to me: *I remember you –*
     you're the one
Who made my dreams come true – just a few – kisses ago. I'm
     taking
One step forward, two steps back, trying to establish what it was
     about her
That made me fall in love with her, if that's what it was;
     infatuation
Was a vogue word then –

It meant it wasn't all quite real. Like looking at my derelict back
     garden,
Its scraggy ranks of docks and nettles, thistles, but thinking
There was something else, flicking idly through the pages of a
     catalogue:
Flowered violets and whites, or grey and silver foliage, sug-
     gesting
Thunderclouds and snowstorms, rivers, fountains; artemesias
     and lilies,
Phlox, gentians, scillas, snowdrops, crocuses; and thymes and
     camomiles
Erupted from the paving-cracks, billowing from half-forgotten
     corners;
An avalanche of jasmine and wisteria broke through. Or, the
     perfume
Of *Blue Grass*, bittersweet, which is, just at this moment, just a
     memory.
How often did she wear it, anyway? I must look her up again
     some day.
And can it still be bought?

For there are memories that have no name; you don't know
     what to ask for.
The merest touch of sunshine, a sudden breeze, might summon
     up
A corner of your life you'd thought, till then, you'd never
     occupied.
Her mother, for example, owned this second-hand shop, which
     is where
The fur coat came from, anonymous with shades of someone
     else. Rummaging
Through piles of coats and dresses, I'd come across a thing that
     until then
I'd never wanted: a white linen 'fifties jacket with no back vent,
Just that bit out of fashion, it was fashionable, or maybe, as they
     say,
It was just the thing I had been looking for. So, a box of worn
     shoes
Might bring me back to 1952, teetering across the kitchen floor
In my mother's high heels –

Not that I wanted to be her; easing off the lid of her powder
     compact,
Breathing in the flesh-coloured dust, was just a way of feeling
     her presence.
And so I have this image of an assignation, where it all comes
     back,
Or nearly all, a long-forgotten kiss: subdued lighting, musak –
     no, a live
Piano – tinkling in its endless loop; there is candlelight and
     Cointreau,
Whispered nothings, as Kathleen Mary Quinlan's *Rhythm*
     meets, across
A discreet table, Calvin Klein's *Obsession*. He has prospered
     since

He saw her last. There is talk of all the years that separated
    them, whatever
Separated them at first. There is talk of money, phrased as talk
    of
Something else, of how there are some things that can't be
    bought
Or maybe it's the name you buy, and not the thing itself.

CIARAN CARSON

A Private Bottling

*So I will go, then. I would rather grieve over your absence
than over you.*
ANTONIO PORCHIA

Back in the same room that an hour ago
we had led, lamp by lamp, into the darkness,
I sit down and turn the radio on low
as the last girl on the planet still awake
reads a dedication to the ships,
and put on a recording of the ocean.

I carefully arrange a chain of nips
in a big fairy-ring; in each square glass
the tincture of a failed geography,
its dwindled burns and woodlands, whin-fires, heather,
the sklent of its wind and its salty rain,
the love-worn habits of its working-folk,
the waveform of their speech, and by extension
how they sing, make love, or take a joke.

So I have a good nose for this sort of thing.

Then I will suffer kiss after fierce kiss,
letting their gold tongues slide along my tongue
as each gives up, in turn, its little song

of the patient years in glass and sherry-oak,
the shy negotiations with the sea,
air and earth, the trick of how the peat-smoke
was shut inside it, like a black thought.

Tonight I toast her with the extinct malts
of Ardlussa, Ladyburn and Dalintober
and an ancient pledge of passionate indifference:
Ochon o do dhoigh me mo chlairsach ar a shon,
wishing her health, as I might wish her weather.

When the circle is closed and I have drunk myself sober
I will tilt the blinds a few degrees, and watch
the dawn grow in a glass of liver-salts,
wait for the birds, the milk-float's sweet nothings,
then slip back to the bed where she lies curled,
replace the live egg of her burning ass
gently in the cold nest of my lap,
as dead to her as she is to the world.

*

Here we are again; it is precisely
twelve, fifteen, thirty years down the road
and one turn higher up the spiral chamber
that separates the burnt ale and dark grains
of what I know, from what I can remember.
Now each glass holds its micro-episode
in permanent suspension, like a movie-frame
on acetate, until it plays again,
revivified by a suave connoisseurship
that deepens in the silence and the dark
to something like an infinite sensitivity.
This is no romantic fantasy: my father
used to know a man who'd taste the sea,
then leave his nets strung out along the bay
because there were no fish in it that day.
Everything is in everything else. It is a matter

of attunement, as once, through the hiss and backwash,
I steered the dial into the voice of God
slightly to the left of Hilversum,
half-drowned by some big, blurry waltz
the way some stars obscure their dwarf companions
for centuries, till someone thinks to look.

In the same way, I can isolate the feints
of feminine effluvia, carrion, shite,
those rogues and toxins only introduced
to give the composition a little weight
as rough harmonics do the violin-note
or Pluto, Cheiron and the lesser saints
might do to our lives, for all you know.
(By Christ, you would recognize their absence
as anyone would testify, having sunk
a glass of *North British*, run off a patent still
in some sleet-hammered satellite of Edinburgh:
a bleak spirit, no amount of caramel
could sweeten or disguise, its after-effect
somewhere between a blanket-bath and a sad wank.
There is, no doubt, a bar in Lothian
where it is sworn upon and swallowed neat
by furloughed riggers and the Special Police,
men who hate the company of women.)

O whiskies of Long Island and Provence!
This little number catches at the throat
but is all sweetness in the finish: my tongue trips
first through burning brake-fluid, then nicotine,
pastis, Diorissimo and wet grass;
another is silk sleeves and lip-service
with a kick like a smacked puss in a train-station;
another, the light charge and the trace of zinc
tap-water picks up at the moon's eclipse.
You will know the time I mean by this.

Because your singular absence, in your absence,
has bred hard, tonight I take the waters
with the whole clan: our faceless ushers, bridesmaids,
our four Shelties, three now ghosts of ghosts;
our douce sons and our lovely loudmouthed daughters
who will, by this late hour, be fully grown,
perhaps with unborn children of their own.
So finally, let me propose a toast:
not to love, or life, or real feeling,
but to their sentimental residue;
to your sweet memory, but not to you.

The sun will close its circle in the sky
before I close my own, and drain that purely
offertory glass that tastes of nothing
but silence, burnt dust on the valves, and whisky.

DON PATERSON

Another Woman

This morning she bought green 'methi'
in the market, choosing the freshest bunch;
picked up a white radish,
imagined the crunch it would make
between her teeth, the sweet sharp taste,
then put it aside, thinking it
an extravagance; counted her coins
out carefully, tied them, a small bundle
into her sari at the waist;
came home, faced her mother-in-law's
dark looks, took
the leaves and chopped them,
her hands stained yellow from the juice;
cut an onion, fine, and cooked
the whole thing in the pot

(salt and cumin seeds thrown in)
over the stove,
shielding her face from the heat.

The usual words came and beat
their wings against her: the money spent,
curses heaped upon her parents,
who had sent her out
to darken other people's doors.

She crouched, as usual, on the floor
beside the stove.
When the man came home
she did not look into his face
nor raise her head, but bent
her back a little more.
Nothing gave her the right
to speak.

She watched the flame hiss up
and beat against the cheap old pot,
a wing of brightness
against its blackened cheek.

This was the house she had been sent to,
the man she had been bound to,
the future she had been born into.

So when the kerosene was thrown
(just a moment of surprise,
a brilliant spark)
it was the only choice
that she had ever known.

Another torch, blazing in the dark.

Another woman.

We shield our faces from the heat.

IMTIAZ DHARKER

Adultery

Wear dark glasses in the rain.
Regard what was unhurt
as though through a bruise.
Guilt. A sick, green tint.

New gloves, money tucked in the palms,
the handshake crackles. Hands
can do many things. Phone.
Open the wine. Wash themselves. Now

you are naked under your clothes all day,
slim with deceit. Only the once
brings you alone to your knees,
miming, more, more, older and sadder,

creative. Suck a lie with a hole in it
on the way home from a lethal, thrilling night
up against a wall, faster. Language
unpeels to a lost cry. You're a bastard.

Do it do it do it. Sweet darkness
in the afternoon; a voice in your ear
telling you how you are wanted,
which way, now. A telltale clock

wiping the hours from its face, your face
on a white sheet, gasping, radiant, yes.
Pay for it in cash, fiction, cab-fares back
to the life which crumbles like a wedding-cake.

Paranoia for lunch; too much
to drink, as a hand on your thigh
tilts the restaurant. You know all about love,
don't you. Turn on your beautiful eyes

for a stranger who's dynamite in bed, again
and again; a slow replay in the kitchen

where the slicing of innocent onions
scalds you to tears. Then, selfish autobiographical sleep

in a marital bed, the tarnished spoon of your body
stirring betrayal, your heart over-ripe at the core.
You're an expert, darling; your flowers
dumb and explicit on nobody's birthday.

So write the script – illness and debt,
a ring thrown away in a garden
no moon can heal, your own words
commuting to bile in your mouth, terror –

and all for the same thing twice. And all
for the same thing twice. You did it.
What. Didn't you. Fuck. Fuck. No. That was
the wrong verb. This is only an abstract noun.

CAROL ANN DUFFY

This Dead Relationship

I carry a dead relationship around everywhere with me.
It's my hobby.
How lucky to have a job that's also my hobby,
To do it all the time.

A few people notice, and ask if they can help carry this thing.
But, like an alcoholic scared they will hear the clink of glass in
    the bag,
I refuse – scared they'll smell rottenness,
Scared of something under their touch
That will cave in, a skin over brown foam on a bad apple.
I cram this thing over the threshold
Into the cold and speechless house,
Lean against the front door for a moment to breathe in the
    dark,

Then start the slow haul to the kitchen.
Steel knives catch the moonlight on white tiles.

This dead relationship.

Or not yet dead.

Or dead and half-eaten,
One eye and one flank open, like a sheep under a hedge.

Or dead but still farting like the bodies in the trenches,
Exploding with their own gas. Hair and nails still growing.

It has the pins and needles of returning feeling in a deadness.
It is a reptile in my hand, quick and small and cool;
The flip of life in a dry, cold bag of loose skin.
A pressure without warmth of small claws and horn moving on
    my palm.

At night it slips slow but purposeful across the floor towards the
    bed.
Next thing it's looking out of my eyes in the morning—
And in the mirror, though my eyes are not my own,
My mouth shows surprise that I am still there at all.

Oh, a sickness that can make you so ill,
Yet doesn't have the decency to kill you.
A mad free-fall that never hits the ground,
Never knows even the relief of sudden shock;
Just endless medium-rare shock, half-firm, half-bloody all the
    time.
A long, slow learning curve.
The overheating that can strip an engine badly,
Strain it far worse than a racing rally.
The fear that you will slow to a stop
Then start a soft, thick, slow-gathering roll backwards.

I want something that is familiar but not.
To feel in someone else's pocket for a key

While they lean away, laughing, their arms up,
Hands in the air covered in grease or dough or paint or clay.

I have to carry it around.
A weeping mother brings a baby to hospital,
Late-night emergency.
The tired doctor smooths the hand-made lace back from its face.
He sees it was stillborn weeks ago, has been dead for weeks.
He looks at her, there is no air in the room...

This dead relationship. This dead and sinking ship.
Bulbs lie, unplanted, on a plate of dust.
Dry and puckered pouches, only slightly mouldy;
Embalmed little stomachs but with hairy, twisted fingers,
Waiting for something to happen without needing to know what
    it is.
When it happens everything else in the universe can start.

This dead relationship.

I am this thing's twin.
One of us is dead
And we don't know which, we are so close.

KATHERINE PIERPOINT

Routine Day Sonnet

For me a perfectly ordinary
day at the office, only a red lorry
past the window at two;
a sailor with a chest tattoo.

A walk before dark
with my daughter to mark
another cross on the papaya tree;
dinner, coffee, bedtime story

of dog, bone and shadow. A bullock cart
in an Eskimo dream. But I wake with a start
to hear my wife cry her heart

out as if from a crater
in hell: she hates me, I hate her,
I'm a filthy rat and a satyr.

A. K. RAMANUJAN

Raymond of the Rooftops

The morning after the night
The roof flew off the house
And our sleeping children narrowly missed
Being decapitated by falling slates,
I asked my husband if he would
Help me put back the roof:
But no – he was too busy at his work
Writing for a women's magazine in London
An Irish Fairytale called *Raymond of the Rooftops*.
Will you have a heart, woman – he bellowed –
Can't you see I am up to my eyes and ears in work,
Breaking my neck to finish *Raymond of the Rooftops*,
Fighting against time to finish *Raymond of the Rooftops*,
Putting everything I have got into *Raymond of the Rooftops*?

Isn't it well for him? *Everything he has got!*

All I wanted him to do was to stand
For an hour, maybe two hours, three at the most,
At the bottom of the stepladder
And hand me up slates while I slated the roof:
But no – once again I was proving to be the insensitive,
Thoughtless, feckless even, wife of the artist.
There was I up to my fat, raw knees in rainwater
Worrying him about the hole in our roof

While he was up to his neck in *Raymond of the Rooftops*.
Will you have a heart, woman – he bellowed –
Can't you see I am up to my eyes and ears in work,
Breaking my neck to finish *Raymond of the Rooftops*,
Fighting against time to finish *Raymond of the Rooftops*,
Putting everything I have got into *Raymond of the Rooftops*?

Isn't it well for him? *Everything he has got!*

PAUL DURCAN

From a Conversation During Divorce

It's cold, you say, the house.
Yes, of course I'll go back one day,
Visit, that is. But the house

Will be cold, just as you say.
Two people have left home,
One of them me, and one

Our youngest child. So of course
It's cold, just as you say,
And big, too, bigger at least

Than it was with everyone there.
Don't think I don't think about you
Being cold in a house that size,

A house that gets bigger, too,
And colder each time I dare
Think about you and the house.

It used to be warm in the days
Before I decided to go,
And it didn't seem big at all,

In fact, it was rather small,
Which is partly the reason I . . .
Don't keep on asking me why

And telling me how it is
In the house. I don't want to know.
How can I go back, how can I

Even visit a house that size,
And getting bigger each minute
With all the cold rooms in it?

CAROL RUMENS

Onions

How easily happiness begins by
dicing onions. A lump of sweet butter
slithers and swirls across the floor
of the sauté pan, especially if its
errant path crosses a tiny slick
of olive oil. Then a tumble of onions.

This could mean soup or risotto
or chutney (from the Sanskrit
chatni, to lick). Slowly the onions
go limp and then nacreous
and then what cookbooks call clear,
though if they were eyes you could see

clearly the cataracts in them.
It's true it can make you weep
to peel them, to unfurl and to tease
from the taut ball first the brittle,
caramel-colored and decrepit
papery outside layer, the least

recent the reticent onion
wrapped around its growing body,
for there's nothing to an onion
but skin, and it's true you can go on
weeping as you go on in, through
the moist middle skins, the sweetest

and thickest, and you can go on
in to the core, to the bud-like,
acrid, fibrous skins densely
clustered there, stalky and in-
complete, and these are the most
pungent, like the nuggets of nightmare

and rage and murmury animal
comfort that infant humans secrete.
This is the best domestic perfume.
You sit down to eat with a rumor
of onions still on your twice-washed
hands and lift to your mouth a hint

of a story about loam and usual
endurance. It's there when you clean up
and rinse the wine glasses and make
a joke, and you leave the minutest
whiff of it on the light switch,
later, when you climb the stairs.

WILLIAM MATTHEWS

Oatmeal

I eat oatmeal for breakfast.
I make it on the hot plate and put skimmed milk on it.
I eat it alone.
I am aware it is not good to eat oatmeal alone.

Its consistency is such that it is better for your mental health if
somebody eats it with you.

That is why I often think up an imaginary companion to have
breakfast with.

Possibly it is even worse to eat oatmeal with an imaginary
companion.

Nevertheless, yesterday morning, I ate my oatmeal – porridge, as
he called it – with John Keats.

Keats said I was absolutely right to invite him: due to its
glutinous texture, gluey lumpishness, hint of slime, and
unusual willingness to disintegrate, oatmeal must never be
eaten alone.

He said that in his opinion, however, it is perfectly OK to eat it
with an imaginary companion,

and he himself had enjoyed memorable porridges with Edmund
Spenser and John Milton.

Even if eating oatmeal with an imaginary companion is not as
wholesome as Keats claims, still, you can learn something
from it.

Yesterday morning, for instance, Keats told me about writing
the 'Ode to a Nightingale'.

He had a heck of a time finishing it – those were his words –
'Oi'ad a 'eck of a toime,' he said, more or less, speaking
through his porridge.

He wrote it quickly, on scraps of paper, which he then stuck in
his pocket,

but when he got home he couldn't figure out the order of the
stanzas, and he and a friend spread the papers on a table,
and they made some sense of them, but he isn't sure to this
day if they got it right.

An entire stanza may have slipped into the lining of his jacket
through a hole in the pocket.

He still wonders about the occasional sense of drift between
stanzas,

and the way here and there a line will go into the configuration
of a Moslem at prayer, then raise itself up and peer about,
and then lay itself down slightly off the mark, causing the
poem to move forward with God's reckless wobble.
He said someone told him that later in life Wordsworth heard
about the scraps of paper on the table, and tried shuffling
some stanzas of his own, but only made matters worse.
I would not have known about any of this but for my reluctance
to eat oatmeal alone.
When breakfast was over, John recited 'To Autumn'.
He recited it slowly, with much feeling, and he articulated the
words lovingly, and his odd accent sounded sweet.
He didn't offer the story of writing 'To Autumn', I doubt if there
is much of one.
But he did say the sight of a just-harvested oat field got him
started on it,
and two of the lines, 'For Summer has o'er-brimmed their
clammy cells' and 'Thou watchest the last oozings hours by
hours', came to him while eating oatmeal alone.
I can see him – drawing a spoon through the stuff, gazing into
the glimmering furrows, muttering – and it occurs to me:
maybe there is no sublime; only the shining of the amnion's
tatters.
For supper tonight I am going to have a baked potato left over
from lunch.
I am aware that a leftover baked potato is damp, slippery, and
simultaneously gummy and crumbly,
and therefore I'm going to invite Patrick Kavanagh to join me.

GALWAY KINNELL

When I Grow Up

When I grow up I want to have a bad leg.
I want to limp down the street I live in
without knowing where I am. I want the disease
where you put your hand on your hip
and lean forward slightly, groaning to yourself.

If a little boy asks me the way
I'll try and touch him between the legs.
What a dirty old man I'm going to be when I grow up!
What shall we do with me?

I promise I'll be good
if you let me fall over in the street
and lie there calling like a baby bird. Please,
nobody come. I'm perfectly all right. I like it here.

I wonder would it be possible
to get me into a National Health Hospice
somewhere in Manchester?
I'll stand in the middle of my cubicle
holding onto a piece of string for safety,
shaking like a leaf at the thought of my suitcase.

I'd certainly like to have a nervous tic
so I can purse my lips up all the time
like Cecil Beaton. Can I be completely bald, please?
I love the smell of old pee.
Why can't I smell like that?

When I grow up I want a thin piece of steel
inserted into my penis for some reason.
Nobody's to tell me why it's there. I want to guess!
Tell me, is that a bottle of old Burgundy
under my bed? I never can tell
if I feel randy any more, can you?

I think it's only fair that I should be allowed
to cough up a bit of blood when I feel like it.
My daughter will bring me a special air cushion
to hold me upright and I'll watch
in baffled admiration as she blows it up for me.

Here's my list: nappies, story books, munchies,
something else. What was the other thing?
I can't remember exactly,
but when I grow up I'll know. When I grow up
I'll pluck at my bedclothes to collect lost thoughts.
I'll roll them into balls and swallow them.

HUGO WILLIAMS

Rat Jelly

See the rat in the jelly
steaming dirty hair
frozen, bring it out on a glass tray
split the pie four ways and eat
I took great care cooking this treat for you
and tho it looks good
and tho it smells of the Westinghouse still
and tastes of exotic fish or
maybe the expensive arse of a cow
I want you to know it's rat
steaming dirty hair and still alive

(caught him last Sunday
thinking of the fridge, thinking of you.)

MICHAEL ONDAATJE

Out West

I was riding one of the best-loved horses in the world.
Hither and yon, we went, here and there,
in and out of the known universe.

'There goes Wild Bill,' people said.
'Look at that varmint go!'
There I went.

I went straight to the dictionary
and looked up varmint.
'What's it say?' said a friend. 'What's it say?'

I thumbed through the pages.
'Vermin,' I said, 'vermin
with an excrescent t.'

'Well doggone,' said someone,
and it's true, the dog was gone,
lost in the gulches and the sages,

leaving just me and the horse,
a couple of ornery critters
who might just as well mosey along,

crossing the ford by starlight,
and miles away, the woman –
lonely and beautiful – waking to find us gone.

BILL MANHIRE

As It Should Be

We hunted the mad bastard
Through bog, moorland, rock, to the star-lit west
And gunned him down in a blind yard
Between ten sleeping lorries
And an electricity generator.

Let us hear no idle talk
Of the moon in the Yellow River;
The air blows softer since his departure.

Since his tide-burial during school hours
Our children have known no bad dreams.
Their cries echo lightly along the coast.

This is as it should be.
They will thank us for it when they grow up
To a world with method in it.

DEREK MAHON

Script Conference

We gotta make a film of this, Jack.
>   *Where's the story?*
It's got everything. Sex. Magic. Despair.
>   *There's no hero.*
There's a part for you in it, Jack. You ride into town.
>   *And ride straight out.*
Jack! It's romantic. Imagine those couples moving closer to
     watch you on late-night TV.
>   *It's no love-story.*
Of course it is. A he & a she. It's terrific!
>   *It is about it.*
At the end you take the girl in your arms. You kiss her. A long,
     shuddering embrace.
>   *She shudders?*
Well, she could die in the end. Or you could meet her at the end
     of the trail.
>   *Six-guns blazing.*
Hey, what kinda story you want? What excites you, Jack?
>   *I like to waltz young women, Benito.*

I know, Jack. Believe me, I know. But this is a movie! It has
   emotion!

                I like to play no emotion.

Whaddaya mean, Jack?

                I like to make a film about
                a shadow in a street. Just a
                shadow. Then you watch it
                crack like a china plate. Very slowly.

That's poetic, Jack! You're a poet! Let's get down to details. The
   old guy is in love with Liza.

                Yeah. He's sitting on the bed.
                Then he leans forward & begins
                to clip his toenails. Close-up.
                Fingers working on toes. About
                five minutes.

We can think about that, Jack. They take the girl away from
   him.

                Or we could show her mouth.
                I'm really interested in that mouth.
                No tongue in it.
                Just that mouth.

Jack! It doesn't exist, the actress with no tongue!

                We could cut it out ourselves.

OK. OK. Jack. Now the marriage. He comes into the church.

                Then we could cut our own
                tongues out.
                We could just stand around.
                Tongueless.

Jack!

                And one final shot.

What's that?

                A man & a woman on a bed.

Good, Jack. That's adult.

                The woman makes weird noises.
                Man groans the same thing over & over.

>   *It's dark.*
>   *Bed begins to whine.*

I don't know if...

>   *The door flies open.*
>   *I just stand there & you have to guess*
>   *who I am.*

Who are you, Jack?

>   *Then nothing happens at all.*
>   *Absolutely nothing.*

It won't sell, Jack. Not in this country.

JOHN HARTLEY WILLIAMS

Aisle of Dogs

In the first cage
a hunk of raw flesh.
No, it was alive, but skinned.

Or its back was skinned.
The knobs of the spine

poked through the bluish meat.

It was a pit bull, held by the shelter
for evidence until the case
could come to trial,

then they'd put him down. The dog,
not the human whose cruelty

lived on in the brindled body,
unmoving except for the enemy eyes.

Not for adoption, said the sign.

All the other cages held adoptable pets,
the manic yappers, sad matted mongrels,
the dumb slobbering abandoned ones,

the sick, the shaved, the scratching,
the wounded and terrified, the lost,

one to a cage, their water dishes
overturned, their shit tracked around,

on both sides of a long echoey
concrete aisle – clank of chain mesh gates,
the attendant hosing down the gutters

with his headphones on, half-dancing
to the song in his head.

I'd come for kittens. There were none.
So I stood in front of the pit bull's
quivering carcass, its longdrawn death,

its untouched food, its incurable hatred
of my species, until the man with the hose
touched my arm and steered me away,

shaking his head in a way that said
Don't look. Leave him alone.
I don't know why, either.

CHASE TWICHELL

On the Venom Farm

I

'My next bite is my last.'
Nine times bitten, Dennis
lifts the lid. Picks out
a Siamese cobra. 'Once bitten
I stay calm. I freeze my mind.
Walk off before it strikes again.
Phone friends. Don was the best
before a mamba got him. Snakes

or scotch. With all of us a toss-up
which gets us first.

'It's never the same. The snake
decides the dose. The last one,
now, the diamondback –
there was a terrible burning.
My vision crazed, like ice.
In thirty minutes I was paralysed.
Sicking up blood. Convulsed.
They 'coptered me to Portsmouth,
ticketed *Dead on Arrival*. My heart
stopped. Can't do that again.

I'm allergic to the serum, see.
I send World Health our milk.
Anti-venom's no more use.
I lost a lot of flesh.'

2

He loves them. When they're ill
he holds them, no gloves,
for the vet. In summer
he climbs into a pit of six

so tourists can see them angry.
We watch smoky knots uncoil.
Hands bare, squeezing the throat-gland,
whipping the tail where he wants it,
he milks the thing into a glass.
'After the snakes, I'm randy.
I tell women they've seen nothing like
a man with cobra in his blood.

A cricket box, though, is essential.'
He flicks the echoing mound

under his trousers. His redhaired wife
serves Margaritas rimmed with salt.

RUTH PADEL

The Sting

Anyone who has ever been hit
straight in the eye by a wasp
knows it's a bit like being poked
by the good Lord's little finger
– it resembles that moment
when the windshield binges
into quartzy toffee
the moment when it's only too clear
– too crystal clear –
that something has broken through
the riotshield that jigs
between self and reality
– it's simply a rehearsal
for the big finger
and it's what happened me
that summer afternoon
near Strabane
though as Tosser McCrossan would say
if thon's all't hit you man
then you're lucky!
or as you might add yourself
I'm sure a wee sting
'll leave your ego still intact
but the fact is
this boy got stung
as we walked by the River Mourne
past Sion Mills
– I was staring at the yellow factory

dozens of windows and windowsills
all summery industry
when that stupid wasp
came zizzing across the river
and ruined my little ploy
for my heart it was set
on the tiny wee hasp
that showed through your cheesecloth blouse
– neither yoghurt nor cheese my love
but sugar brown sugar brown sugar
– but we couldn't dive down in the grass
for my sudden new patch of flesh
was hardly a turn-on that day
– just imagine
there'd have reared above you
the small bare ass
of that closed that stretched eyelid
blind and bald like a scaldy
or some indignant vulture
– *wouldn't you rather go back to the house?*
but as we continued our dander
you seemed relieved
and I felt – well – shrived
it was a pilgrimage of a kind
as we left that plonky
invented village behind
pushing through shives
of chippy sunlight
and the birds' *sip sip sip*
you with your brown lovely skin
me with my carrion eye
– then across the river
happened this curtainless manse
with a collapsed stone wall
and an orchard
all lichened and neglected

except that from out it the air
suthered a ripeness of plums
across the wimpling water
I closed my good eye
– what brushed my unkissed lips
like a prayer
was the blue grapes of Gilead

TOM PAULIN

Raptor

You have made God small,
setting him astride
a pipette or a retort
studying the bubbles,
absorbed in an experiment
that will come to nothing.

I think of him rather
as an enormous owl
abroad in the shadows,
brushing me sometimes
with his wing so the blood
in my veins freezes, able

to find his way from one
soul to another because
he can see in the dark.
I have heard him crooning
to himself, so that almost
I could believe in angels,

those feathered overtones
in love's rafters, I have heard
him scream, too, fastening
his talons in his great

adversary, or in some lesser
denizen, maybe, like you or me.

R. S. THOMAS

From the Childhood of Jesus

One Saturday morning he went to the river to play.
He modeled twelve sparrows out of the river clay

And scooped a clear pond, with a dam of twigs and mud.
Around the pond he set the birds he had made,

Evenly as the hours. Jesus was five. He smiled,
As a child would who had made a little world

Of clear still water and clay beside a river.
But a certain Jew came by, a friend of his father

And he scolded the child and ran at once to Joseph,
Saying, 'Come see how your child has profaned the Sabbath,

Making images at the river on the Day of Rest.'
So Joseph came to the place and took his wrist

And told him, 'Child, you have offended the Word.'
Then Jesus freed the hand that Joseph held

And clapped his hands and shouted to the birds
To go away. They raised their beaks at his words

And breathed and stirred their feathers and flew away.
The people were frightened. Meanwhile, another boy,

The son of Annas the scribe, had idly taken
A branch of driftwood and leaning against it had broken

The dam and muddied the little pond and scattered
The twigs and stones. Then Jesus was angry and shouted,

'Unrighteous, impious, ignorant, what did the water
Do to harm you? Now you are going to wither

The way a tree does, you shall bear no fruit
And no leaves, you shall wither down to the root.'

At once, the boy was all withered. His parents moaned,
The Jews gasped, Jesus began to leave, then turned

And prophesied, his child's face wet with tears:
'Twelve times twelve times twelve thousands of years

Before these heavens and this earth were made,
The Creator set a jewel in the throne of God

With Hell on the left and Heaven to the right,
The Sanctuary in front, and behind, an endless night

Endlessly fleeing a Torah written in flame.
And on that jewel in the throne, God wrote my name.'

Then Jesus left and went into Joseph's house.
The family of the withered one also left the place,

Carrying him home. The Sabbath was nearly over.
By dusk, the Jews were all gone from the river.

Small creatures came from the undergrowth to drink
And foraged in the shadows along the bank.

Alone in his cot in Joseph's house, the Son
Of Man was crying himself to sleep. The moon

Rose higher, the Jews put out their lights and slept,
And all was calm and as it had been, except

In the agitated household of the scribe Annas,
And high in the dark, where unknown even to Jesus

The twelve new sparrows flew aimlessly through the night,
Not blinking or resting, as if never to alight.

ROBERT PINSKY

You Will Know When You Get There

Nobody comes up from the sea as late as this
in the day and the season, and nobody else goes down

the last steep kilometre, wet-metalled where
a shower passed shredding the light which keeps

pouring out of its tank in the sky, through summits,
trees, vapours thickening and thinning. Too

credibly by half celestial, the dammed
reservoir up there keeps emptying while the light lasts

over the sea, where it 'gathers the gold against
it'. The light is bits of crushed rock randomly

glinting underfoot, wetted by the short
shower, and down you go and so in its way does

the sun which gets there first. Boys, two of them,
turn campfirelit faces, a hesitancy to speak

is a hesitancy of the earth rolling back and away
behind this man going down to the sea with a bag

to pick mussels, having an arrangement with the tide,
the ocean to be shallowed three point seven metres,

one hour's light to be left and there's the excrescent
moon sponging off the last of it. A door

slams, a heavy wave, a door, the sea-floor shudders.
Down you go alone, so late, into the surge-black fissure.

ALLEN CURNOW

Caliban's Books

Hair oil, boiled sweets, chalk dust, squid's ink...
Bear with me. I'm trying to conjure my father,
age fourteen, as Caliban – picked by Mr Quinn
for the role he was born to play because
'I was the handsomest boy at school'
he'll say, straight-faced, at fifty.
This isn't easy. I've only half the spell,
and I won't be born for twenty years.
I'm trying for rainlight on Belfast Lough
and listening for a small blunt accent barking
over the hiss of a stove getting louder like surf.
But how can I read when the schoolroom's gone
black as the hold of a ship? Start again.

Hair oil, boiled sweets...
But his paperbacks are crumbling in my hands,
sea-changed bouquets, each brown page
scribbled on, underlined, memorized,
forgotten like used pornography:
The Pocket Treasury of English Verse
How to Win Friends and Influence People
30 Days to a More Powerful Vocabulary

Fish stink, pitch stink, seaspray, cedarwood...
I seem to have brought us to the port of Naples,
midnight, to a shadow below deck
dreaming of a distant island.
So many years, so many ports ago!
The moment comes. It slips from the hold
and knucklewalks across the dark piazza
sobbing, *maestro! maestro!* But the duke's long dead
and all his magic books are drowned.

MICHAEL DONAGHY

The Draft Horse

With a lantern that wouldn't burn
In too frail a buggy we drove
Behind too heavy a horse
Through a pitch-dark limitless grove.

And a man came out of the trees
And took our horse by the head
And reaching back to his ribs
Deliberately stabbed him dead.

The ponderous beast went down
With a crack of a broken shaft.
And the night drew through the trees
In one long invidious draft.

The most unquestioning pair
That ever accepted fate
And the least disposed to ascribe
Any more than we had to to hate,

We assumed that the man himself
Or someone he had to obey
Wanted us to get down
And walk the rest of the way.

ROBERT FROST

Why Brownlee Left

Why Brownlee left, and where he went,
Is a mystery even now.
For if a man should have been content
It was him; two acres of barley,
One of potatoes, four bullocks,
A milker, a slated farmhouse.

He was last seen going out to plough
On a March morning, bright and early.

By noon Brownlee was famous;
They had found all abandoned, with
The last rig unbroken, his pair of black
Horses, like man and wife,
Shifting their weight from foot to
Foot, and gazing into the future.

PAUL MULDOON

Street

He fell in love with the butcher's daughter
When he saw her passing by in her white trousers
Dangling a knife on a ring at her belt.
He stared at the dark shining drops on the paving-stones.

One day he followed her
Down the slanting lane at the back of the shambles.
A door stood half-open
And the stairs were brushed and clean,
Her shoes paired on the bottom step,
Each tread marked with the red crescent
Her bare heels left, fading to faintest at the top.

EILÉAN NÍ CHUILLEANÁIN

The Other

She had too much so with a smile you took some.
Of everything she had you had
Absolutely nothing, so you took some.
At first, just a little.

Still she had so much she made you feel
Your vacuum, which nature abhorred,
So you took your fill, for nature's sake.
Because her great luck made you feel unlucky
You had redressed the balance, which meant
Now you had some too, for yourself.
As seemed only fair. Still her ambition
Claimed the natural right to screw you up
Like a crossed-out page, tossed into a basket.
Somebody, on behalf of the gods,
Had to correct that hubris.
A little touch of hatred steadied the nerves.

Everything she had won, the happiness of it,
You collected
As your compensation
For having lost. Which left her absolutely
Nothing. Even her life was
Trapped in the heap you took. She had nothing.
Too late you saw what had happened.
It made no difference that she was dead.
Now that you had all she had ever had
You had much too much.
                         Only you
Saw her smile, as she took some.
At first, just a little.

TED HUGHES

Not Waving but Drowning

Nobody heard him, the dead man,
But still he lay moaning:
I was much further out than you thought
And not waving but drowning.

Poor chap, he always loved larking
And now he's dead
It must have been too cold for him his heart gave way,
They said.

Oh, no no no, it was too cold always
(Still the dead one lay moaning)
I was much too far out all my life
And not waving but drowning.

STEVIE SMITH

Skunk Hour

for Elizabeth Bishop

Nautilus Island's hermit
heiress still lives through winter in her Spartan cottage;
her sheep still graze above the sea.
Her son's a bishop. Her farmer
is first selectman in our village,
she's in her dotage.

Thirsting for
the hierarchic privacy
of Queen Victoria's century,
she buys up all
the eyesores facing her shore,
and lets them fall.

The season's ill—
we've lost our summer millionaire,
who seemed to leap from an L. L. Bean
catalogue. His nine-knot yawl
was auctioned off to lobstermen.
A red fox stain covers Blue Hill.

And now our fairy
decorator brightens his shop for fall,
his fishnet's filled with orange cork,
orange, his cobbler's bench and awl,
there is no money in his work,
he'd rather marry.

One dark night,
my Tudor Ford climbed the hill's skull,
I watched for love-cars. Lights turned down,
they lay together, hull to hull,
where the graveyard shelves on the town...
My mind's not right.

A car radio bleats,
'Love, O careless Love...' I hear
my ill-spirit sob in each blood cell,
as if my hand were at its throat...
I myself am hell,
nobody's here—

only skunks, that search
in the moonlight for a bite to eat.
They march on their soles up Main Street:
white stripes, moonstruck eyes' red fire
under the chalk-dry and spar spire
of the Trinitarian Church.

I stand on top
of our back steps and breathe the rich air—
a mother skunk with her column of kittens swills the garbage
    pail.
She jabs her wedge head in a cup
of sour cream, drops her ostrich tail,
and will not scare.

ROBERT LOWELL

The Old Fools

What do they think has happened, the old fools,
To make them like this? Do they somehow suppose
It's more grown-up when your mouth hangs open and drools,
And you keep on pissing yourself, and can't remember
Who called this morning? Or that, if they only chose,
They could alter things back to when they danced all night,
Or went to their wedding, or sloped arms some September?
Or do they fancy there's really been no change,
And they've always behaved as if they were crippled or tight,
Or sat through days of thin continuous dreaming
Watching light move? If they don't (and they can't), it's
   strange:
         Why aren't they screaming?

At death, you break up: the bits that were you
Start speeding away from each other for ever
With no one to see. It's only oblivion, true:
We had it before, but then it was going to end,
And was all the time merging with a unique endeavour
To bring to bloom the million-petalled flower
Of being here. Next time you can't pretend
There'll be anything else. And these are the first signs:
Not knowing how, not hearing who, the power
Of choosing gone. Their looks show that they're for it:
Ash hair, toad hands, prune face dried into lines –
         How can they ignore it?

Perhaps being old is having lighted rooms
Inside your head, and people in them, acting.
People you know, yet can't quite name; each looms
Like a deep loss restored, from known doors turning,
Setting down a lamp, smiling from a stair, extracting
A known book from the shelves; or sometimes only
The rooms themselves, chairs and a fire burning,
The blown bush at the window, or the sun's

Faint friendliness on the wall some lonely
Rain-ceased midsummer evening. That is where they live:
Not here and now, but where all happened once.
              This is why they give

An air of baffled absence, trying to be there
Yet being here. For the rooms grow farther, leaving
Incompetent cold, the constant wear and tear
Of taken breath, and them crouching below
Extinction's alp, the old fools, never perceiving
How near it is. This must be what keeps them quiet:
The peak that stays in view wherever we go
For them is rising ground. Can they never tell
What is dragging them back, and how it will end? Not at night?
Not when the strangers come? Never, throughout
The whole hideous inverted childhood? Well,
              We shall find out.

PHILIP LARKIN

I Go Back to May 1937

I see them standing at the formal gates of their colleges,
I see my father strolling out
under the ochre sandstone arch, the
red tiles glinting like bent
plates of blood behind his head, I
see my mother with a few light books at her hip
standing at the pillar made of tiny bricks with the
wrought-iron gate still open behind her, its
sword-tips black in the May air,
they are about to graduate, they are about to get married,
they are kids, they are dumb, all they know is they are
innocent, they would never hurt anybody.
I want to go up to them and say Stop,

don't do it – she's the wrong woman,
he's the wrong man, you are going to do things
you cannot imagine you would ever do,
you are going to do bad things to children,
you are going to suffer in ways you never heard of,
you are going to want to die. I want to go
up to them there in the late May sunlight and say it,
her hungry pretty blank face turning to me,
her pitiful beautiful untouched body,
his arrogant handsome blind face turning to me,
his pitiful beautiful untouched body,
but I don't do it. I want to live. I
take them up like the male and female
paper dolls and bang them together
at the hips like chips of flint as if to
strike sparks from them, I say
Do what you are going to do, and I will tell about it.

SHARON OLDS

You Hated Spain

               Spain frightened you. Spain
Where I felt at home. The blood-raw light,
The oiled anchovy faces, the African
Black edges to everything, frightened you.
Your schooling had somehow neglected Spain.
The wrought-iron grille, death and the Arab drum.
You did not know the language, your soul was empty
Of the signs, and the welding light
Made your blood shrivel. Bosch
Held out a spidery hand and you took it
Timidly, a bobby-sox American.
You saw right down to the Goya funeral grin
And recognized it, and recoiled

As your poems winced into chill, as your panic
Clutched back towards college America.
So we sat as tourists at the bullfight
Watching bewildered bulls awkwardly butchered,
Seeing the grey-faced matador, at the barrier
Just below us, straightening his bent sword
And vomiting with fear. And the horn
That hid itself inside the blowfly belly
Of the toppled picador punctured
What was waiting for you. Spain
Was the land of your dreams: the dust-red cadaver
You dared not wake with, the puckering amputations
No literature course had glamorized.
The juju land behind your African lips.
Spain was what you tried to wake up from
And could not. I see you, in moonlight,
Walking the empty wharf at Alicante
Like a soul waiting for the ferry,
A new soul, still not understanding,
Thinking it is still your honeymoon
In the happy world, with your whole life waiting,
Happy, and all your poems still to be found.

TED HUGHES

An October Salmon

He's lying in poor water, a yard or so depth of poor safety,
Maybe only two feet under the no-protection of an outleaning
        small oak,
Half under a tangle of brambles.

After his two thousand miles, he rests,
Breathing in that lap of easy current
In his graveyard pool.

About six pounds weight,
Four years old at most, and a bare winter at sea –
But already a veteran,
Already a death-patched hero. So quickly it's over!

So briefly he roamed the gallery of marvels!
Such sweet months, so richly embroidered into earth's beauty-
    dress,
Her life-robe –
Now worn out with her tirelessness, her insatiable quest,
Hangs in the flow, a frayed scarf –

An autumnal pod of his flower,
The mere hull of his prime, shrunk at shoulder and flank,

With the sea-going Aurora Borealis of his April power –
The primrose and violet of that first upfling in the estuary –
Ripened to muddy dregs,
The river reclaiming his sea-metals.

In the October light
He hangs there, patched with leper-cloths.

Death has already dressed him
In her clownish regimentals, her badges and decorations,
Mapping the completion of his service,
His face a ghoul-mask, a dinosaur of senility, and his whole
    body
A fungoid anemone of canker –

Can the caress of water ease him?
The flow will not let up for a minute.

What a change! From that covenant of Polar Light
To this shroud in a gutter!
What a death-in-life – to be his own spectre!
His living body become death's puppet!
Dolled by death in her crude paints and drapes
He haunts his own staring vigil

And suffers the subjection, and the dumbness,
And the humiliation of the role!

And that is how it is,
That is what is going on there, under the scrubby oak tree,
     hour after hour,
That is what the splendour of the sea has come down to,
And the eye of ravenous joy – king of infinite liberty
In the flashing expanse, the bloom of sea-life,

On the surge-ride of energy, weightless,
Body simply the armature of energy
In that earliest sea-freedom, the savage amazement of life,
The salt mouthful of actual existence
With strength like light –

Yet this was always with him. This was inscribed in his egg.
This chamber of horrors is also home.
He was probably hatched in this very pool.
And this was the only mother he ever had, this uneasy channel
     of minnows
Under the mill-wall, with bicycle wheels, car-tyres, bottles
And sunk sheets of corrugated iron.
People walking their dogs trail their evening shadows across
     him.
If boys see him they will try to kill him.

All this, too, is stitched into the torn richness,
The epic poise
That holds him so steady in his wounds, so loyal to his doom,
     so patient
In the machinery of heaven.

TED HUGHES

Notations of Ten Summer Minutes

A boy skips flat stones out to sea – each does fine
till a small wave meets it head on and swallows it.
The boy will do the same.

The schoolmaster stands looking out of the window
with one Latin eye and one Greek one.
A boat rounds the point in Gaelic.

Out of the shop comes a stream
of Omo, Weetabix, BiSoDol tablets and a man
with a pocket shaped like a whisky bottle.

Lord V. walks by with the village in his pocket.
Angus walks by
spending the village into the air.

A melodeon is wheezing a clear-throated jig
on the deck on the *Arcadia*. On the shore hills Pan
cocks a hairy ear; and falls asleep again.

The ten minutes are up, except they aren't.
I leave the village, except I don't.
The jig fades to silence, except it doesn't.

NORMAN MACCAIG

Soap Suds

This brand of soap has the same smell as once in the big
House he visited when he was eight: the walls of the bathroom
    open
To reveal a lawn where a great yellow ball rolls back through a
    hoop
To rest at the head of a mallet held in the hands of a child.

And these were the joys of that house: a tower with a
    telescope;
Two great faded globes, one of the earth, one of the stars;
A stuffed black dog in the hall; a walled garden with bees;
A rabbit warren; a rockery; a vine under glass; the sea.

To which he has now returned. The day of course is fine
And a grown-up voice cries Play! The mallet slowly swings,
Then crack, a great gong booms from the dog-dark hall and
    the ball
Skims forward through the hoop and then through the next
    and then

Through hoops where no hoops were and each dissolves in
    turn
And the grass has grown head-high and an angry voice cries
    Play!
But the ball is lost and the mallet slipped long since from the
    hands
Under the running tap that are not the hands of a child.

LOUIS MACNEICE

A Sofa in the Forties

All of us on the sofa in a line, kneeling
Behind each other, eldest down to youngest,
Elbows going like pistons, for this was a train

And between the jamb-wall and the bedroom door
Our speed and distance were inestimable.
First we shunted, then we whistled, then

Somebody collected the invisible
For tickets and very gravely punched it
As carriage after carriage under us

Moved faster, *chooka-chook*, the sofa legs
Went giddy and the unreachable ones
Far out on the kitchen floor began to wave.

*

Ghost-train? Death-gondola? The carved, curved ends,
Black leatherette and ornate gauntness of it
Made it seem the sofa had achieved

Flotation. Its castors on tip-toe,
Its braid and fluent backboard gave it airs
Of superannuated pageantry:

When visitors endured it, straight-backed,
When it stood off in its own remoteness,
When the insufficient toys appeared on it

On Christmas mornings, it held out as itself,
Potentially heavenbound, earthbound for sure,
Among things that might add up or let you down.

*

We entered history and ignorance
Under the wireless shelf. *Yippee-i-ay*,
Sang 'The Riders of the Range'. HERE IS THE NEWS,

Said the absolute speaker. Between him and us
A great gulf was fixed where pronunciation
Reigned tyrannically. The aerial wire

Swept from a treetop down in through a hole
Bored in the windowframe. When it moved in wind,
The sway of language and its furtherings

Swept and swayed in us like nets in water
Or the abstract, lonely curve of distant trains
As we entered history and ignorance.

*

holding your head down
until every bubble of breath
is squeezed from your lungs

and the flat leaves and spiky flowers
float over you like a wreath.
I sit on the stones until I'm numb,

until, among reflections of sky,
water-buttercups, spears of iris,
your face rises to the surface –

a face that was always puffy
and pale, so curiously unchanged.
A wind rocks the waxy flowers, curls

the edges of the leaves. Blue dragonflies
appear and vanish like ghosts.
I part the mats of yellow weed

and drag you to the bank, covering
your green algae-stained corpse
with a white sheet. Then, I lift the edge

and climb in underneath –
humping your chest,
breathing into your mouth.

    VICKI FEAVER

Houdini

is not clear how he entered me
  why he always has to escape.
aybe he's just proving to the crowds
  can still do it – He whispers
lf-words which bloom in the dark
a ha ma ha.

We occupied our seats with all our might,
Fit for the uncomfortableness.
Constancy was its own reward already.

Out in front, on the big upholstered arm,
Somebody craned to the side, driver or
Fireman, wiping his dry brow with the air

Of one who had run the gauntlet. We were
The last thing on his mind, it seemed; we sensed
A tunnel coming up where we'd pour through

Like unlit carriages through fields at night,
Our only job to sit, eyes straight ahead,
And be transported and make engine noise.

    SEAMUS HEANEY

Ancient Evenings

for A.

My friends hunted in packs, had themselves photographed
under hoardings that said 'Tender Vegetables'
or 'Big Chunks', but I had you – my Antonia!
Not for long, nor for a long time now ...

Later, your jeans faded more completely,
and the hole in them wore to a furred square,
as it had to, but I remember my hands
skating over them, there where the cloth was thickest.

You were so quiet, it seemed like an invitation
to be disturbed, like Archimedes and the soldier,
like me, like the water displaced from my kettle
when I heated tins of viscous celery soup in it

until the glue dissolved and the labels crumbled
and the turbid, overheated water turned into more soup ...

I was overheated, too. I could not trust my judgement.
The coffee I made in the dark was eight times too strong.

My humour was gravity, so I sat us both in an armchair
and toppled over backwards. I must have hoped
the experience of danger would cement our relationship.
Nothing was broken, and we made surprisingly little noise.

MICHAEL HOFMANN

My Second Marriage to My First Husband

We married for acceptance: to stall the nagging
married friends who wanted us
to do it there and then –
with them. In the downy wedlocked bed
we ask 'Is there life after
one-day honeymoons to Kissamee Springs?
Was I all right?' The answers, woefully,
are no and no. And yes,

we lollygagged down the aisle, vowed
to forsake dallying, shilly-shallying, and cleave
only onto one another, to forever romp
in the swampy rumpus
room of our eccentricities: that sanctum
sanctorum where I sport
bedsocks and never rise
till noon. What did we know?
Did you know my love for animals
has always been acute? Perhaps in time
I will become a shepherdess, a jockey.

At the reception every table was adorned
with toilet tissue cy-
cloned into swans. When I unraveled one
to find the charm, the management

was shocked. Dismembering swans!
No bride had ever ... And the prize, a little gizzard
of a ring, was disappointing. Oh Person,

was it worth it? Of course,
we fit at dinner parties. But as one part warbles
to be normal, another puts a spin on things.
I see you striving to frolic
in your steel-mesh tweeds as I model
chiffon voluptuaries the color of exhaust.

In the wedding album we end or commence
our revels. There we are! doing the cha-cha-cha
to the boom-chick-chick band
in our dyed-to-match togs.
We're getting fat
on the eats, foaming
white crumbs, 'Honey' and 'Dear'
cumbersome as live doves
on our tongues.

Bring squeezeboxes, gardenias,
a hybrid of the two. Congratulate us,
chums. Smile and freeze: our dimples stiffen
to resolute framed stares. How adult
we look! Our eyes burn
stoplights in the Instamatic squares.

ALICE FULTON

Lily Pond

Thinking of new ways to kill you
and bring you back from the dead,
I try drowning you in the lily pond –

And these were the joys of that house: a tower with a
    telescope;
Two great faded globes, one of the earth, one of the stars;
A stuffed black dog in the hall; a walled garden with bees;
A rabbit warren; a rockery; a vine under glass; the sea.

To which he has now returned. The day of course is fine
And a grown-up voice cries Play! The mallet slowly swings,
Then crack, a great gong booms from the dog-dark hall and
    the ball
Skims forward through the hoop and then through the next
    and then

Through hoops where no hoops were and each dissolves in
    turn
And the grass has grown head-high and an angry voice cries
    Play!
But the ball is lost and the mallet slipped long since from the
    hands
Under the running tap that are not the hands of a child.

LOUIS MACNEICE

A Sofa in the Forties

All of us on the sofa in a line, kneeling
Behind each other, eldest down to youngest,
Elbows going like pistons, for this was a train

And between the jamb-wall and the bedroom door
Our speed and distance were inestimable.
First we shunted, then we whistled, then

Somebody collected the invisible
For tickets and very gravely punched it
As carriage after carriage under us

Moved faster, *chooka-chook*, the sofa legs
Went giddy and the unreachable ones
Far out on the kitchen floor began to wave.

*

Ghost-train? Death-gondola? The carved, curved ends,
Black leatherette and ornate gauntness of it
Made it seem the sofa had achieved

Flotation. Its castors on tip-toe,
Its braid and fluent backboard gave it airs
Of superannuated pageantry:

When visitors endured it, straight-backed,
When it stood off in its own remoteness,
When the insufficient toys appeared on it

On Christmas mornings, it held out as itself,
Potentially heavenbound, earthbound for sure,
Among things that might add up or let you down.

*

We entered history and ignorance
Under the wireless shelf. *Yippee-i-ay*,
Sang 'The Riders of the Range'. HERE IS THE NEWS,

Said the absolute speaker. Between him and us
A great gulf was fixed where pronunciation
Reigned tyrannically. The aerial wire

Swept from a treetop down in through a hole
Bored in the windowframe. When it moved in wind,
The sway of language and its furtherings

Swept and swayed in us like nets in water
Or the abstract, lonely curve of distant trains
As we entered history and ignorance.

*

We occupied our seats with all our might,
Fit for the uncomfortableness.
Constancy was its own reward already.

Out in front, on the big upholstered arm,
Somebody craned to the side, driver or
Fireman, wiping his dry brow with the air

Of one who had run the gauntlet. We were
The last thing on his mind, it seemed; we sensed
A tunnel coming up where we'd pour through

Like unlit carriages through fields at night,
Our only job to sit, eyes straight ahead,
And be transported and make engine noise.

SEAMUS HEANEY

Ancient Evenings

for A.

My friends hunted in packs, had themselves photographed
under hoardings that said 'Tender Vegetables'
or 'Big Chunks', but I had you – my Antonia!
Not for long, nor for a long time now…

Later, your jeans faded more completely,
and the hole in them wore to a furred square,
as it had to, but I remember my hands
skating over them, there where the cloth was thickest.

You were so quiet, it seemed like an invitation
to be disturbed, like Archimedes and the soldier,
like me, like the water displaced from my kettle
when I heated tins of viscous celery soup in it

until the glue dissolved and the labels crumbled
and the turbid, overheated water turned into more soup…

I was overheated, too. I could not trust my judgement.
The coffee I made in the dark was eight times too strong.

My humour was gravity, so I sat us both in an armchair
and toppled over backwards. I must have hoped
the experience of danger would cement our relationship.
Nothing was broken, and we made surprisingly little noise.

MICHAEL HOFMANN

My Second Marriage to My First Husband

We married for acceptance: to stall the nagging
married friends who wanted us
to do it there and then –
with them. In the downy wedlocked bed
we ask 'Is there life after
one-day honeymoons to Kissamee Springs?
Was I all right?' The answers, woefully,
are no and no. And yes,

we lollygagged down the aisle, vowed
to forsake dallying, shilly-shallying, and cleave
only onto one another, to forever romp
in the swampy rumpus
room of our eccentricities: that sanctum
sanctorum where I sport
bedsocks and never rise
till noon. What did we know?
Did you know my love for animals
has always been acute? Perhaps in time
I will become a shepherdess, a jockey.

At the reception every table was adorned
with toilet tissue cy-
cloned into swans. When I unraveled one
to find the charm, the management

was shocked. Dismembering swans!
No bride had ever ... And the prize, a little gizzard
of a ring, was disappointing. Oh Person,

was it worth it? Of course,
we fit at dinner parties. But as one part warbles
to be normal, another puts a spin on things.
I see you striving to frolic
in your steel-mesh tweeds as I model
chiffon voluptuaries the color of exhaust.

In the wedding album we end or commence
our revels. There we are! doing the cha-cha-cha
to the boom-chick-chick band
in our dyed-to-match togs.
We're getting fat
on the eats, foaming
white crumbs, 'Honey' and 'Dear'
cumbersome as live doves
on our tongues.

Bring squeezeboxes, gardenias,
a hybrid of the two. Congratulate us,
chums. Smile and freeze: our dimples stiffen
to resolute framed stares. How adult
we look! Our eyes burn
stoplights in the Instamatic squares.

ALICE FULTON

Lily Pond

Thinking of new ways to kill you
and bring you back from the dead,
I try drowning you in the lily pond –

holding your head down
until every bubble of breath
is squeezed from your lungs

and the flat leaves and spiky flowers
float over you like a wreath.
I sit on the stones until I'm numb,

until, among reflections of sky,
water-buttercups, spears of iris,
your face rises to the surface—

a face that was always puffy
and pale, so curiously unchanged.
A wind rocks the waxy flowers, curls

the edges of the leaves. Blue dragonflies
appear and vanish like ghosts.
I part the mats of yellow weed

and drag you to the bank, covering
your green algae-stained corpse
with a white sheet. Then, I lift the edge

and climb in underneath—
thumping your chest,
breathing into your mouth.

VICKI FEAVER

Houdini

It is not clear how he entered me
or why he always has to escape.
Maybe he's just proving to the crowds
he can still do it – He whispers
half-words which bloom in the dark
Ma ha ma ha.

Sometimes he feeds me cough medicine.
Or bathes his genitals in salt water.
Then heaves his body upwards
as if pressing against a lid.
At least he prefers me
to his underwater box, to the manacles
which clank on his moon-white skin.
I wonder what it is exactly
he sees within me?
He touches my insides as though
he'd sighted the first landplants –
I'm catching cloud between my fingers.

Tonight the wind whips through my stomach
over knots of trees and sharp rocks.
When he rushes out of me the crowd gasps –
and I implode from sheer emptiness.

MONIZA ALVI

In Your Mind

The other country, is it anticipated or half-remembered?
Its language is muffled by the rain which falls all afternoon
one autumn in England, and in your mind
you put aside your work and head for the airport
with a credit card and a warm coat you will leave
on the plane. The past fades like newsprint in the sun.

You know people there. Their faces are photographs
on the wrong side of your eyes. A beautiful boy
in the bar on the harbour serves you a drink – what? –
asks you if men could possibly land on the moon.
A moon like an orange drawn by a child. No.
Never. You watch it peel itself into the sea.

Sleep. The rasp of carpentry wakes you. On the wall,
a painting lost for thirty years renders the room yours.
Of course. You go to your job, right at the old hotel, left,
then left again. You love this job. Apt sounds
mark the passing of the hours. Seagulls. Bells. A flute
practising scales. You swap a coin for a fish on the way home

Then suddenly you are lost but not lost, dawdling
on the blue bridge, watching six swans vanish
under your feet. The certainty of place turns on the lights
all over town, turns up the scent on the air. For a moment
you are there, in the other country, knowing its name.
And then a desk. A newspaper. A window. English rain.

CAROL ANN DUFFY

Love from a Foreign City

Dearest, the cockroaches are having babies.
One fell from the ceiling into my gin
with no ill effects. Mother has been.
I showed her the bite marks on the cot
and she gave me the name of her rat-catcher.
He was so impressed by the hole in her u-bend,
he took it home for his personal museum.
I cannot sleep. They are digging up children
on Hackney Marshes. The papers say
when that girl tried to scream for help,
the man cut her tongue out. Not far from here.
There have been more firebombs,
but only at dawn and out in the suburbs.
And a mortar attack. We heard it from the flat,
a thud like someone dropping a table.
They say the pond life coming out of the taps
is completely harmless. A law has been passed
on dangerous dogs: muzzles, tattoos, castration.

When the labrador over the road jumped up
to say hello to Billie, he wet himself.
The shops in North End Road are all closing.
You can't get your shoes mended anywhere.
The one-way system keeps changing direction,
I get lost a hundred yards from home.
There are parts of the new *A to Z* marked simply
'under development'. Even street names
have been demolished. There is typhoid in Finchley.
Mother has brought me a lavender tree.

LAVINIA GREENLAW

The Letter

If I remember right, his first letter.
Found where? My side-plate perhaps,
or propped on our heavy brown tea-pot.
One thing is clear – my brother leaning
across asking *Who is he?* half angry
as always that summer before enlistment.

Then alone in the sunlit yard, mother
unlocking a door to call *Up so early?*
– waving her yellow duster goodbye
in a small sinking cloud. The gate creaks
shut and there in the lane I am running
uphill, vanishing where the woodland starts.

The Ashground. A solid contour swept
through ripening wheat, and fringe
of stippled green shading the furrow.
Now I am hardly breathing, gripping
the thin paper and reading *Write to me.*
Write to me please. I miss you. My angel.

Almost shocked, but repeating him line
by line, and watching the words jitter
under the pale spidery shadows of leaves.
How else did I leave the plane unheard
so long? But suddenly there it was—
a Messerschmitt low at the wood's edge.

What I see today is the window open,
the pilot's unguarded face somehow
closer than possible. Goggles pushed up,
a stripe of ginger moustache, and his eyes
fixed on my own while I stand
with the letter held out, my frock blowing,

before I am lost in cover again,
heading for home. He must have banked
at once, climbing steeply until his jump
and watching our simple village below—
the Downs swelling and flattening, speckled
with farms and bushy chalk-pits. By lunch

they found where he lay, the parachute
tight in its pack, and both hands spread
as if they could break the fall. I still
imagine him there exactly. His face pressed
close to the sweet-smelling grass. His legs
splayed wide in a candid unshamable V.

ANDREW MOTION

Looking Up

The hot air balloon convention floats
above our garden – weeks pass
but no one wants to come down.
At first the firemen stood by, ready
with their longest ladders,

their life nets and jumping sheets.
But now they've taken off
in their own, fire-red hot air balloons:
giant fireballs that dare to compete with the sun.
Who can look after the roses when the sky
ripples and throbs with so much passion?
Our neighbour's attic window glitters balloon-mad
and nostalgic for another life.
Yesterday's sunflower stares and stares.
The birch trees twitch restless
and can't get rid of their spores.
Only the children speak gently
as they collect snails
and line them up along the stone wall.

SUJATA BHATT

Knot

Let me do to you what they do
to the dead – now, while you are still
alive, your blank moon face hanging
half-empty, as if begging.

Let me wash and fill you
with soft white stuff, feed cotton
into your loose cheeks, gather
your jaw shut with silk chiffon.

Let me do it to you now,
paint my cosmetic sunset
across your cheekbones, comfort
your tired eyelids with pennies.

Later, when you die, we can
cut through silk, let the face fly

open, the scarf shake out
its map of escaping creases, as we

roll wet swabs between us
like picnic eggs, the familiar
bag flapping, the small change
jingling again in our purses.

SUSAN WICKS

Small Female Skull

With some surprise, I balance my small female skull in my
    hands.
What is it like? An ocarina? Blow in its eye.
It cannot cry, holds my breath only as long as I exhale,
mildly alarmed now, into the hole where the nose was,
press my ear to its grin. A vanishing sigh.

For some time, I sit on the lavatory seat with my head
in my hands, appalled. It feels much lighter than I'd thought;
the weight of a deck of cards, a slim volume of verse,
but with something else, as though it could levitate. Disturbing.
So why do I kiss it on the brow, my warm lips to its papery
    bone,

and take it to the mirror to ask for a gottle of geer?
I rinse it under the tap, watch dust run away, like sand
from a swimming-cap, then dry it – firstborn – gently
with a towel. I see the scar where I fell for sheer love
down treacherous stairs, and read that shattering day like
    braille.

Love, I murmur to my skull, then, louder, other grand words,
shouting the hollow nouns in a white-tiled room.
Downstairs they will think I have lost my mind. No. I only
    weep

into these two holes here, or I'm grinning back at the joke, this
   is
a friend of mine. See, I hold her face in trembling, passionate
   hands.

CAROL ANN DUFFY

Green Sees Things in Waves

Green first thing each day sees waves —
the chair, armoire, overhead fixtures, you name it,
waves — which, you might say, things really are,
but Green just lies there awhile breathing
long slow breaths, in and out, through his mouth
like he was maybe seasick, until in an hour or so
the waves simmer down and then the trails and colours
off of things, that all quiets down as well and Green
starts to think of washing up, breakfast even
with everything still moving around, colours, trails
and sounds, from the street and plumbing next door,
vibrating — of course you might say that's what
sound really is, after all, vibrations — but Green
he's not thinking physics at this stage, nuh-uh,
our boy's only trying to get himself out of bed,
get a grip, but sometimes, and this is the kicker,
another party, shall we say, is in the room
with Green, and Green knows this other party
and they do *not* get along, which understates it
quite a bit, quite a bit, and Green knows
that this other cat is an hallucination, right,
but these two have a routine that goes way back
and Green starts hollering, throwing stuff
until he's all shook up, whole day gone to hell,
bummer...

Anyhow, the docs are having a look,
see if they can't dream up a cocktail,
but seems our boy ate quite a pile of acid one time,
clinical, wow, enough juice for half a block –
go go go, little Greenie – blew the wiring out
from behind his headlights and now, no matter what,
can't find the knob to turn off the show.

AUGUST KLEINZAHLER

Two Hangovers

Number One

I slouch in bed.
Beyond the streaked trees of my window,
All groves are bare.
Locusts and poplars change to unmarried women
Sorting slate from anthracite
Between railroad ties:
The yellow-bearded winter of the depression
Is still alive somewhere, an old man
Counting his collection of bottle caps
In a tarpaper shack under the cold trees
Of my grave.

I still feel half drunk,
And all those old women beyond my window
Are hunching toward the graveyard.

Drunk, mumbling Hungarian,
The sun staggers in,
And his big stupid face pitches
Into the stove.
For two hours I have been dreaming
Of green butterflies searching for diamonds
In coal seams;

And children chasing each other for a game
Through the hills of fresh graves.
But the sun has come home drunk from the sea,
And a sparrow outside
Sings of the Hanna Coal Co. and the dead moon.
The filaments of cold light bulbs tremble
In music like delicate birds.
Ah, turn it off.

Number Two:
I Try to Waken and Greet the World Once Again

In a pine tree,
A few yards away from my window sill,
A brilliant blue jay is springing up and down, up and down,
On a branch.

I laugh, as I see him abandon himself
To entire delight, for he knows as well as I do
That the branch will not break.

JAMES WRIGHT

Death of a Poet

Suddenly his mouth filled with sand.
His tractor of blood stopped thumping.
He held five icicles in each hand.
His heart packed up jumping.

His face turned the colour of something forgotten in the larder.
His thirty-two teeth were expelled on the kitchen floor.
His muscles, at long last, got considerably harder.
He felt younger than he had for some time before.

Four heroes, steady as wrestlers, each carried him on a
shoulder
Into a great grey church laid out like a brain.

An iron bowl sent out stiff rays of chrysanthemums. It grew
  colder.
The sun, as expected, failed to break through the pane.

The parson boomed like a dockyard gun at a christening.
Somebody read from the bible. It seemed hours.
I got the feeling you were curled up inside the box, listening.
There was the thud of hymn-books, the stench of flowers.

I remembered hearing your voice on a bloody foment
Of Atlantic waters. The words burned clear as a flare.
Life begins, you said, *as of this moment*.
A bird flew down out of the hurling air.

Over the church a bell broke like a wave upended.
The hearse left for winter with a lingering hiss.
I looked in the wet sky for a sign, but no bird descended.
I went across the road to the pub; wrote this.

CHARLES CAUSLEY

Memento Mori

There is no need for me to keep a skull on my desk,
to stand with one foot up on the ruins of Rome,
or to wear a locket with a sliver of a saint's bone.

It is enough to realize that every common object
in this small sunny room will outlive me—
the mirror, radio, bookstand and rocker.

Not one of these things will attend my burial,
not even this battered gooseneck lamp
with its steady, silent benediction of light,

though I could put worse things in my mind
than the image of it waddling across the cemetery
like an old servant, dragging the tail of its cord,
the small circle of mourners parting to make room.

BILLY COLLINS

Death of an Irishwoman

Ignorant, in the sense
she ate monotonous food
and thought the world was flat,
and pagan, in the sense
she knew the things that moved
all night were neither dogs nor cats
but púcas and darkfaced men
she nevertheless had fierce pride.
But sentenced in the end
to eat thin diminishing porridge
in a stone-cold kitchen
she clenched her brittle hands
around a world
she could not understand.
I loved her from the day she died.
She was a summer dance at the crossroads.
She was a cardgame where a nose was broken.
She was a song that nobody sings.
She was a house ransacked by soldiers.
She was a language seldom spoken.
She was a child's purse, full of useless things.

MICHAEL HARTNETT

Cups

They know us by our lips. They know the proverb
about the space between us. Many slip.
They are older than their flashy friends, the glasses.
They held cold water first, are named in scripture.

Most are gregarious. You'll often see them
nestled in snowy flocks on trestle tables
or perched on trolleys. Quite a few stay married
for life in their own home to the same saucer,

and some are virgin brides of quietness
in a parlour cupboard, wearing gold and roses.
Handleless, chipped, some live on in the flour bin,
some with the poisons in the potting shed.

Shattered, they lie in flowerpot, flowerbed, fowlyard.
Fine earth in earth, they wait for resurrection.
Restored, unbreakable, they'll meet our lips
on some bright morning filled with lovingkindness.

GWEN HARWOOD

Hospital Evening

Sunset: the blaze of evening burns
through curtains like a firelit ghost.
Kröte, dreaming of snow, returns
to something horrible on toast

slapped at him by a sulky nurse
whose boyfriend's waiting. Kröte loves
food. Is this food? He finds it worse
than starving, as he cuts and shoves

one nauseating mouthful down.
Kröte has managed to conceal

some brandy in his dressing gown.
He gulps it fast, until the real

sunset's a field of painted light
and his white curtains frame a stage
where he's the hero and must fight
his fever. He begins to rage

fortissimo in German, flings
the empty bottle on the floor;
roars for more brandy, thumps and sings.
Three nurses crackle through the door

and hold him down. He struggles, then
submits to the indignities
nurses inflict, and sleeps again,
dreaming he goes, where the stiff trees

glitter in silence, hand in hand
with a young child he does not know,
who walking makes no footprint and
no shadow on soft-fallen snow.

GWEN HARWOOD

The Hospital

A year ago I fell in love with the functional ward
Of a chest hospital: square cubicles in a row
Plain concrete, wash basins – an art lover's woe,
Not counting how the fellow in the next bed snored.

But nothing whatever is by love debarred,
The common and banal her heat can know.
The corridor led to a stairway and below
Was the inexhaustible adventure of a gravelled yard.

This is what love does to things: the Rialto Bridge,
The main gate that was bent by a heavy lorry,
The seat at the back of a shed that was a suntrap.
Naming these things is the love-act and its pledge;
For we must record love's mystery without claptrap,
Snatch out of time the passionate transitory.

PATRICK KAVANAGH

The Tune the Old Cow Died of

'The tune the old cow died of,'
My grandmother used to say
When my uncle played the flute.
She hadn't seen a cow for many a day,
Shut in by slate
Walls that bound her
To scullery and yard and soot-
blackened flowerpots and hart's-tongue fern.
She watched her fourteen sons grow up around her
In a back street,
Blocked at one end by crags of slag,
Barred at the other by the railway goods-yard gate.
The toot of the flute
Piped to a parish where never cow could earn
Her keep – acres of brick
With telegraph poles and chimneys reared up thick
As ricks in a harvest field.
My grandmother remembered
Another landscape where the cattle
Waded halfway to the knees
In swish of buttercup and yellow rattle,
And un-shorn, parasite-tormented sheep
Flopped down like grey bolsters in the shade of trees,
And the only sound

Was the whine of a hound
In the out-of-hunting-season summer,
Or the cheep of wide-beaked, new-hatched starlings,
Or the humdrum hum of the bees.

Then

A cow meant milk, meant cheese, meant money,
And when a cow died
With foot-and-mouth or wandered out on the marshes
And drowned at the high tide,
The children went without whatever their father had promised.
When she was a girl
There was nothing funny,
My grandmother said,
About the death of a cow,
And it isn't funny now
To millions hungrier even than she was then.
So when the babies cried,
One after each for over fourteen years,
Or the flute squeaked at her ears,
Or the council fire-alarm let off a scream
Like steam out of a kettle and the whole mad town
Seemed fit to blow its lid off – she could find
No words to ease her mind
Like those remembered from her childhood fears:
'The tune the old cow died of.'

NORMAN NICHOLSON

What Work Is

We stand in the rain in a long line
waiting at Ford Highland Park. For work.
You know what work is – if you're
old enough to read this you know what
work is, although you may not do it.

Forget you. This is about waiting,
shifting from one foot to another.
Feeling the light rain falling like mist
into your hair, blurring your vision
until you think you see your own brother
ahead of you, maybe ten places.
You rub your glasses with your fingers,
and of course it's someone else's brother,
narrower across the shoulders than
yours but with the same sad slouch, the grin
that does not hide the stubbornness,
the sad refusal to give in to
rain, to the hours wasted waiting,
to the knowledge that somewhere ahead
a man is waiting who will say, 'No,
we're not hiring today,' for any
reason he wants. You love your brother,
now suddenly you can hardly stand
the love flooding you for your brother,
who's not beside you or behind or
ahead because he's home trying to
sleep off a miserable night shift
at Cadillac so he can get up
before noon to study his German.
Works eight hours a night so he can sing
Wagner, the opera you hate most,
the worst music ever invented.
How long has it been since you told him
you loved him, held his wide shoulders,
opened your eyes wide and said those words,
and maybe kissed his cheek? You've never
done something so simple, so obvious,
not because you're too young or too dumb,
not because you're jealous or even mean
or incapable of crying in

the presence of another man, no,
just because you don't know what work is.

PHILIP LEVINE

The Patriot

I am standing for peace and non-violence.
Why world is fighting fighting
Why all people of world
Are not following Mahatma Gandhi,
I am simply not understanding.
Ancient Indian Wisdom is 100% correct.
I should say even 200% correct.
But Modern generation is neglecting –
Too much going for fashion and foreign thing.

Other day I'm reading in newspaper
(Every day I'm reading *Times of India*
To improve my English Language)
How one goonda fellow
Throw stone at Indirabehn.
Must be student unrest fellow, I am thinking.
Friends, Romans, Countrymen, I am saying (to myself)
Lend me the ears.
Everything is coming –
Regeneration, Remuneration, Contraception.
Be patiently, brothers and sisters.

You want one glass lassi?
Very good for digestion.
With little salt lovely drink,
Better than wine;
Not that I am ever tasting the wine.
I'm the total teetotaller, completely total.
But I say
Wine is for the drunkards only.

[251]

What you think of prospects of world peace?
Pakistan behaving like this,
China behaving like that,
It is making me very sad, I am telling you.
Really, most harassing me.
All men are brothers, no?
In India also
Gujaraties, Maharashtrians, Hindiwallahs
All brothers—
Though some are having funny habits.
Still, you tolerate me,
I tolerate you,
One day Ram Rajya is surely coming.

You are going?
But you will visit again
Any time, any day,
I am not believing in ceremony.
Always I am enjoying your company.

NISSIM EZEKIEL

The Second Voyage

Odysseus rested on his oar and saw
The ruffled foreheads of the waves
Crocodiling and mincing past: he rammed
The oar between their jaws and looked down
In the simmering sea where scribbles of weed defined
Uncertain depth, and the slim fishes progressed
In fatal formation, and thought

                          If there was a single
Streak of decency in these waves now, they'd be ridged
Pocked and dented with the battering they've had,
And we could name them as Adam named the beasts,
Saluting a new one with dismay, or a notorious one

With admiration; they'd notice us passing
And rejoice at our shipwreck, but these
Have less character than sheep and need more patience.

I know what I'll do he said;
I'll park my ship in the crook of a long pier
(And I'll take you with me he said to the oar)
I'll face the rising ground and walk away
From tidal waters, up riverbeds
Where herons parcel out the miles of stream,
Over gaps in the hills, through warm
Silent valleys, and when I meet a farmer
Bold enough to look me in the eye
With 'where are you off to with that long
Winnowing fan over your shoulder?'
There I will stand still
And I'll plant you for a gatepost or a hitching-post
And leave you as a tidemark. I can go back
And organize my house then.
                      But the profound
Unfenced valleys of the ocean still held him;
He had only the oar to make them keep their distance;
The sea was still frying under the ship's side.
He considered the water-lilies, and thought about fountains
Spraying as wide as willows in empty squares,
The sugarstick of water clattering into the kettle,
The flat lakes bisecting the rushes. He remembered spiders and
    frogs
Housekeeping at the roadside in brown trickles floored with
    mud,
Horsetroughs, the black canal, pale swans at dark:
His face grew damp with tears that tasted
Like his own sweat or the insults of the sea.

EILÉAN NÍ CHUILLEANÁIN

The Sea

It used to be at the bottom of the hill
and brought white ships and news
of a far land where half my life
was scheduled to be lived.

That was at least half a life ago
of managing without maps, plans, permanence
of a dozen or more addresses
of riding the trains like a vagrant.

Today, I have visitors. They come
long distances overland. They will be uneasy
and console me for loss of the sea.
I will discourage them.

E. A. MARKHAM

The Birth

Seven o'clock. The seventh day of the seventh month of the
    year.
No sooner have I got myself up in lime-green scrubs,
a sterile cap and mask,
and taken my place at the head of the table

than the windlass-women ply their shears
and gralloch-grub
for a footling foot, then, warming to their task,
haul into the inestimable

realm of apple-blossoms and chanterelles and damsons and eel-
    spears
and foxes and the general hubbub
of inkies and jennets and Kickapoos with their lemniscs
or peekaboo-quiffs of Russian sable

and tallow-unctuous vernix, into the realm of the widgeon –
the 'whew' or 'yellow-poll', not the 'zuizin' –

Dorothy Aoife Korelitz Muldoon: I watch through floods of
    tears
as they give her a quick rub-a-dub
and whisk
her off to the nursery, then check their staple-guns for staples.

PAUL MULDOON

Balloons

Since Christmas they have lived with us,
Guileless and clear,
Oval soul-animals,
Taking up half the space,
Moving and rubbing on the silk

Invisible air drifts,
Giving a shriek and pop
When attacked, then scooting to rest, barely trembling.
Yellow cathead, blue fish –
Such queer moons we live with

Instead of dead furniture!
Straw mats, white walls
And these travelling
Globes of thin air, red, green,
Delighting

The heart like wishes or free
Peacocks blessing
Old ground with a feather
Beaten in starry metals.
Your small

Brother is making
His balloon squeak like a cat.
Seeming to see
A funny pink world he might eat on the other side of it,
He bites,

Then sits
Back, fat jug
Contemplating a world clear as water.
A red
Shred in his little fist.

SYLVIA PLATH

The King of the Cats Is Dead

The light on his thigh was like
a waterfall in Iceland, and his hair
was the tidal rip between two rocks,
his claws retracted sat in softness
deeper than the ancient moss of Blarney,
his claws extended were the coulter
of the gods and a raw March wind
was in his merely agricultural yawn.
Between his back legs was a catapult
of fecundity and he was riggish
as a red-haired man. The girls
of our nation felt him brush their legs
when they were bored with telling rosaries –
at night he clawed their brains in their
coffined beds and his walnut mind
wrinkled on their scalps. His holidays
were upside down in water and then
his face was like the sun: his smell
was in the peat smoke and even his midden
was a harmony of honey. When he stalked

his momentary mice the land shook
as though Atlantic waves were bowling
at the western walls. But his eyes
were the greatest thing about him.
They burned low and red so that drunks
saw them like two stars above a hedge,
they held the look of last eyes
in a drowning man, they were the sight
the rebel angels saw the first morning
of expulsion. And he is dead – a voice
from the centre of the earth told of his death
by treachery, that he lies in a hole
of infamy, his kidneys and his liver
torn from his body.
                              Therefore tell
the men and horses of the market-place,
the swallows laying twigs, the salmon
on the ladder that nothing is
as it has been
                      time is explored
and all is known, the portents
are of brief and brutal things, since
all must hear the words of desolation,
The King of the Cats is Dead
                                      and it
is only Monday in the world.

PETER PORTER

The Broad Bean Sermon

Beanstalks, in any breeze, are a slack church parade
without belief, saying *trespass against us* in unison,
recruits in mint Air Force dacron, with unbuttoned leaves.

Upright with water like men, square in stem-section
they grow to great lengths, drink rain, keel over all ways,
kink down and grow up afresh, with proffered new greenstuff.

Above the cat-and-mouse floor of a thin bean forest
snails hang rapt in their food, ants hurry through several
    dimensions,
spiders tense and sag like little black flags in their cordage.

Going out to pick beans with the sun high as fence-tops, you
    find
plenty, and fetch them. An hour or a cloud later
you find shirtfulls more. At every hour of daylight

appear more that you missed: ripe, knobbly ones, fleshy-sided,
thin-straight, thin-crescent, frown-shaped, bird-shouldered,
    boat-keeled ones,
beans knuckled and single-bulged, minute green dolphins at
    suck,

beans upright like lecturing, outstretched like blessing fingers
in the incident light, and more still, oblique to your notice
that the noon glare or cloud-light or afternoon slants will
    uncover

till you ask yourself Could I have overlooked so many, or
do they form in an hour? unfolding into reality
like templates for subtly broad grins, like unique caught
    expressions,

like edible meanings, each sealed around with a string
and affixed to its moment, an unceasing colloquial assembly,
the portly, the stiff, and those lolling in pointed green
    slippers...

Wondering who'll take the spare bagfulls, you grin with
        happiness
– it is your health – you vow to pick them all
even the last few, weeks off yet, misshapen as toes.

LES MURRAY

Homecoming

All day, day after day, they're bringing them home,
they're picking them up, those they can find, and bringing them
        home,
they're bringing them in, piled on the hulls of Grants, in trucks,
        in convoys,
they're zipping them up in green plastic bags,
they're tagging them now in Saigon, in the mortuary coolness
they're giving them names, they're rolling them out of
the deep-freeze lockers – on the tarmac at Tan Son Nhut
the noble jets are whining like hounds,
they are bringing them home
– curly-heads, kinky-hairs, crew-cuts, balding non-coms
– they're high, now, high and higher, over the land, the
        steaming *chow mein*,
their shadows are tracing the blue curve of the Pacific
with sorrowful quick fingers, heading south, heading east,
home, home, home – and the coasts swing upward, the old
        ridiculous curvatures
of earth, the knuckled hills, the mangrove-swamps, the desert
        emptiness...
in their sterile housing they tilt towards these like skiers
– taxiing in, on the long runways, the howl of their
        homecoming rises
surrounding them like their last moments (the mash, the
        splendour)
then fading at length as they move

on to small towns where dogs in the frozen sunset
raise muzzles in mute salute,
and on to cities in whose wide web of suburbs
telegrams tremble like leaves from a wintering tree
and the spider grief swings in his bitter geometry
– they're bringing them home, now, too late, too early.

BRUCE DAWE

Fifteen Million Plastic Bags

I was walking in a government warehouse
Where the daylight never goes.
I saw fifteen million plastic bags
Hanging in a thousand rows.

Five million bags were six feet long
Five million were five foot five
Five million were stamped with Mickey Mouse
And they came in a smaller size.

Were they for guns or uniforms
Or a dirty kind of party game?
Then I saw each bag had a number
And every bag bore a name.

And five million bags were six feet long
Five million were five foot five
Five million were stamped with Mickey Mouse
And they came in a smaller size

So I've taken my bag from the hanger
And I've pulled it over my head
And I'll wait for the priest to zip it
So the radiation won't spread

Now five million bags are six feet long
Five million are five foot five
Five million are stamped with Mickey Mouse
And they come in a smaller size.

ADRIAN MITCHELL

Presidents

What a joy to climb into bed
being the President of the United States
knowing that probably countless thousands
of even your non-psychotic fellow citizens
are dreaming about you all over the republic.
From Fescue Meadows, Oregon,
to Utility Mills, Massachusetts,
they keep dreaming about you
and your good looks.
At a remote substation in the Valley of Fire,
Assistant Inspector Lloyd E. Towner, Jr.,
has fallen asleep
in a green and yellow lawn-chair
in the only pool of shade
behind the only building in southeast Nevada.
He is dreaming of Anasazi demons
with enormous hands and feet
and penises like snub-nosed revolvers
and testicles brassy as spittoons
and faces full of clacking tongues
that tell him: Inform the President
that we are ready
to extinguish the Evils
he names for us one by one.
In the next frame it is 1948 again.
It is Mrs Sterling's class in kindergarten.

We have just completed our versions
of George Washington causing the daily war
in purple crayon on slick pieces of paper.

MICHAEL HEFFERNAN

Portraits of Tudor Statesmen

Surviving is keeping your eyes open,
Controlling the twitchy apparatus
Of iris, white, cornea, lash and lid.

So the literal painter set it down –
The sharp raptorial look; strained eyeball;
And mail, ruff, bands, beard, anything, to hide
The violently vulnerable neck.

U. A. FANTHORPE

Not My Best Side

I

Not my best side, I'm afraid.
The artist didn't give me a chance to
Pose properly, and as you can see,
Poor chap, he had this obsession with
Triangles, so he left off two of my
Feet. I didn't comment at the time
(What, after all, are two feet
To a monster?) but afterwards
I was sorry for the bad publicity.
Why, I said to myself, should my conqueror
Be so ostentatiously beardless, and ride
A horse with a deformed neck and square hoofs?
Why should my victim be so

Unattractive as to be inedible,
And why should she have me literally
On a string? I don't mind dying
Ritually, since I always rise again,
But I should have liked a little more blood
To show they were taking me seriously.

II

It's hard for a girl to be sure if
She wants to be rescued. I mean, I quite
Took to the dragon. It's nice to be
Liked, if you know what I mean. He was
So nicely physical, with his claws
And lovely green skin, and that sexy tail,
And the way he looked at me,
He made me feel he was all ready to
Eat me. And any girl enjoys that.
So when this boy turned up, wearing machinery,
On a really *dangerous* horse, to be honest,
I didn't much fancy him. I mean,
What was he like underneath the hardware?
He might have acne, blackheads or even
Bad breath for all I could tell, but the dragon –
Well, you could see all his equipment
At a glance. Still, what could I do?
The dragon got himself beaten by the boy,
And a girl's got to think of her future.

III

I have diplomas in Dragon
Management and Virgin Reclamation.
My horse is the latest model, with
Automatic transmission and built-in
Obsolescence. My spear is custom-built,
And my prototype armour

Still on the secret list. You can't
Do better than me at the moment.
I'm qualified and equipped to the
Eyebrow. So why be difficult?
Don't you want to be killed and/or rescued
In the most contemporary way? Don't
You want to carry out the roles
That sociology and myth have designed for you?
Don't you realize that, by being choosy,
You are endangering job-prospects
In the spear- and horse-building industries?
What, in any case, does it matter what
You want? You're in my way.

U. A. FANTHORPE

My Belovèd Compares Herself to a Pint of Stout

When in the heat of the first night of summer
I observe with a whistle of envy
That Jackson has driven out the road for a pint of stout,
She puts her arm around my waist and scolds me:
Am I not your pint of stout? Drink me.
There is nothing except, of course, self-pity
To stop you also having your pint of stout.

Putting self-pity on a leash in the back of the car,
I drive out the road, do a U-turn,
Drive in the hall door, up the spiral staircase,
Into her bedroom. I park at the foot of her bed,
Nonchalantly step out leaving the car unlocked,
Stroll over to the chest of drawers, lean on it,
Circumspectly inspect the backs of my hands,
Modestly request from her a pint of stout.
She turns her back, undresses, pours herself into bed,
Adjusts the pillows, slaps her hand on the coverlet:

Here I am – at the very least
Look at my new cotton nightdress before you shred it
And do not complain that I have not got a head on me.

I look around to see her foaming out of the bedclothes
Not laughing but gazing at me out of four-leggèd eyes.
She says: Close your eyes, put your hands around me.
I am the blackest, coldest pint you will ever drink
So sip me slowly, let me linger on your lips,
Ooze through your teeth, dawdle down your throat,
Before swooping down into your guts.
While you drink me I will deposit my scum
On your rim and when you get to the bottom of me,
No matter how hard you try to drink my dregs –
And being a man, you will, no harm in that –
I will keep bubbling up back at you.
For there is no escaping my aftermath.
Tonight – being the first night of summer –
You may drink as many pints of me as you like.
There are barrels of me in the tap room.
In thin daylight at nightfall,
You will fall asleep drunk on love.
When you wake early in the early morning
You will have a hangover,
All chaste, astringent, aflame with affirmation,
Straining at the bit to get to first mass
And holy communion and work – the good life.

PAUL DURCAN

Margin Prayer from an Ancient Psalter

Lord I know, and I know you know I know
this is a drudge's penance. Only dull scholars
or cowherds maddened with cow-watching
will ever read *The Grey Psalter of Antrim*.

I have copied it these thirteen years
waiting for the good bits – High King of the Roads,
are there any good bits in *The Grey Psalter of Antrim*?

(Text illegible here because of teeth-marks.)

It has the magic realism of an argumentum:
it has the narrative subtlety of the Calendar of Oengus;
it has the oblique wit of the Battle-Cathach of the O'Donnells;
it grips like the colophon to The Book of Durrow;
it deconstructs like a canon-table;
it makes St Jerome's Defence of his Vulgate look racy.
I would make a gift of it to Halfdane the Sacker
that he might use it to wipe his wide Danish arse.
Better its volumes intincted our cattle-trough
and cured poor Luke, my three-legged calf,
than sour my wit and spoil my calligraphy.
Luke! White Luke! Truer beast than Ciarán's Dun Cow!
You would rattle the abbot with your soft off-beats
butting his churns and licking salt from his armpits.
Luke, they flayed you, pumiced your skin to a wafer –
such a hide as King Tadhg might die under –
for pages I colour with ox-gall yellow . . .

(Text illegible here because of tear-stains.)

Oh Forgiving Christ of scribes and sinners
intercede for me with the jobbing abbot!
Get me re-assigned to something pagan
with sex and perhaps gratuitous violence
which I might deplore with insular majuscule
and illustrate with Mozarabic complexity
Ad maioram gloriam Dei et Hiberniae,
and lest you think I judge the book too harshly
from pride or a precious sensibility
I have arranged for a second opinion.
Tomorrow our surveyor, Ronan the Barbarian,
will read out loud as only he can read out loud

selected passages from this which I have scored
while marking out his new church in Killaney
in earshot of that well-versed man, King Suibhne...

(Text completely illegible from this point
because of lake-water damage and otter dung.)

IAN DUHIG

The Lion for Real

Soyez muette pour moi, Idole contemplative...

I came home and found a lion in my living room
Rushed out on the fire-escape screaming Lion! Lion!
Two stenographers pulled their brunette hair and banged the
    window shut
I hurried home to Paterson and stayed two days.

Called up my old Reichian analyst
who'd kicked me out of therapy for smoking marijuana
'It's happened' I panted 'There's a Lion in my room'
'I'm afraid any discussion would have no value' he hung up.

I went to my old boyfriend we got drunk with his girlfriend
I kissed him and announced I had a lion with a mad gleam in my
    eye
We wound up fighting on the floor I bit his eyebrow & he kicked
    me out
I ended masturbating in his jeep parked in the street moaning
    'Lion.'

Found Joey my novelist friend and roared at him 'Lion!'
He looked at me interested and read me his spontaneous ignu
    high poetries

I listened for lions all I heard was Elephant Tiglon Hippogryph
    Unicorn Ants
But figured he really understood me when we made it in Ignaz
    Wisdom's bathroom.

But next day he sent me a leaf from his Smokey Mountain
    retreat
'I love you little Bo-Bo with your delicate golden lions
But there being no Self and No Bars therefore the Zoo of your
    dear Father hath no Lion
You said your mother was mad don't expect me to produce the
    Monster for your Bridegroom.'

Confused dazed and exalted bethought me of real lion starved
    in his stink in Harlem
Opened the door the room was filled with the bomb blast of
    his anger
He roaring hungrily at the plaster walls but nobody could hear
    him outside thru the window
My eye caught the edge of the red neighbor apartment building
    standing in deafening stillness

We gazed at each other his implacable yellow eye in the red
    halo of fur
Waxed rheumy on my own but he stopped roaring and bared a
    fang greeting.
I turned my back and cooked broccoli for supper on an iron
    gas stove
boilt water and took a hot bath in the old tub under the sink
    board.

He didn't eat me, tho I regretted him starving in my presence.
Next week he wasted away a sick rug full of bones wheaten
    hair falling out
enraged and reddening eye as he lay aching huge hairy head on
    his paws
by the egg-crate bookcase filled up with thin volumes of Plato,
    & Buddha.

Sat by his side every night averting my eyes from his hungry
　　motheaten face
stopped eating myself he got weaker and roared at night while
　　I had nightmares
Eaten by lion in bookstore on Cosmic Campus, a lion myself
　　starved by Professor Kandisky, dying in a lion's flophouse
　　circus,
I woke up mornings the lion still added dying on the floor –
　　'Terrible Presence!' I cried 'Eat me or die!'

It got up that afternoon – walked to the door with its paw on
　　the wall to steady its trembling body
Let out a soul rending creak from the bottomless roof of his
　　mouth
thundering from my floor to heaven heavier than a volcano at
　　night in Mexico
Pushed the door open and said in a gravelly voice 'Not this
　　time Baby – but I will be back again.'

Lion that eats my mind now for a decade knowing only your
　　hunger
Not the bliss of your satisfaction O roar of the Universe how
　　am I chosen
In this life I have heard your promise I am ready to die I have
　　served
Your starved and ancient Presence O Lord I wait in my room
　　at your Mercy.

ALLEN GINSBERG

Underwear

I didn't get much sleep last night
thinking about underwear
Have you ever stopped to consider
underwear in the abstract

When you really dig into it
some shocking problems are raised
Underwear is something
we all have to deal with
Everyone wears
some kind of underwear
Even Indians
wear underwear
Even Cubans
wear underwear
The Pope wears underwear I hope
The Governor of Louisiana
wears underwear
I saw him on TV
He must have had tight underwear
He squirmed a lot
Underwear can really get you in a bind
You have seen the underwear ads
for men and women
so alike but so different
Women's underwear holds things up
Men's underwear holds things down
Underwear is one thing
men and women have in common
Underwear is all we have between us
You have seen the three-color pictures
with crotches encircled
to show the areas of extra strength
and three-way stretch
promising full freedom of action
Don't be deceived
It's all based on the two-party system
which doesn't allow much freedom of choice
the way things are set up
America in its Underwear
struggles thru the night

Underwear controls everything in the end
Take foundation garments for instance
They are really fascist forms
of underground government
making people believe
something but the truth
telling you what you can or can't do
Did you ever try to get around a girdle
Perhaps Non-Violent Action
is the only answer
Did Gandhi wear a girdle?
Did Lady Macbeth wear a girdle?
Was that why Macbeth murdered sleep?
And that spot she was always rubbing —
Was it really in her underwear?
Modern anglosaxon ladies
must have huge guilt complexes
always washing and washing and washing
Out damned spot
Underwear with spots very suspicious
Underwear with bulges very shocking
Underwear on clothesline a great flag of freedom
Someone has escaped his Underwear
May be naked somewhere
Help!
But don't worry
Everybody's still hung up in it
There won't be no real revolution
And poetry still the underwear of the soul
And underwear still covering
a multitude of faults
in the geological sense —
strange sedimentary stones, inscrutable cracks!
If I were you I'd keep aside
an oversize pair of winter underwear
Do not go naked into that good night

And in the meantime
keep calm and warm and dry
No use stirring ourselves up prematurely
'over Nothing'
Move forward with dignity
hand in vest
Don't get emotional
And death shall have no dominion
There's plenty of time my darling
Are we not still young and easy
Don't shout

LAWRENCE FERLINGHETTI

Black Silk

She was cleaning – there is always
that to do – when she found,
at the top of the closet, his old
silk vest. She called me
to look at it, unrolling it carefully
like something live
might fall out. Then we spread it
on the kitchen table and smoothed
the wrinkles down, making our hands
heavy until its shape against formica
came back and the little tips
that would have pointed to his pockets
lay flat. The buttons were all there.
I held my arms out and she
looped the wide armholes over
them. 'That's one thing I never
wanted to be,' she said, 'a man.'
I went into the bathroom to see
how I looked in the sheen and

sadness. Wind chimes
off-key in the alcove. Then her
crying so I stood back in the sink-light
where the porcelain had been staring. Time
to go to her, I thought, with that
other mind, and stood still.

TESS GALLAGHER

A True Account of Talking to the Sun at Fire Island

The Sun woke me this morning loud
and clear, saying 'Hey! I've been
trying to wake you up for fifteen
minutes. Don't be so rude, you are
only the second poet I've ever chosen
to speak to personally

                  so why
aren't you more attentive? If I could
burn you through the window I would
to wake you up. I can't hang around
here all day.'

              'Sorry, Sun, I stayed
up late last night talking to Hal.'

'When I woke up Mayakovsky he was
a lot more prompt' the Sun said
petulantly. 'Most people are up
already waiting to see if I'm going
to put in an appearance.'

                    I tried
to apologize 'I missed you yesterday.'
'That's better' he said. 'I didn't
know you'd come out.' 'You may be
wondering why I've come so close?'
'Yes' I said beginning to feel hot

wondering if maybe he wasn't burning me
anyway.

       'Frankly I wanted to tell you
I like your poetry. I see a lot
on my rounds and you're okay. You may
not be the greatest thing on earth, but
you're different. Now, I've heard some
say you're crazy, they being excessively
calm themselves to my mind, and other
crazy poets think that you're a boring
reactionary. Not me.

               Just keep on
like I do and pay no attention. You'll
find that people always will complain
about the atmosphere, either too hot
or too cold too bright or too dark, days
too short or too long.

              If you don't appear
at all one day they think you're lazy
or dead. Just keep right on, I like it.

And don't worry about your lineage
poetic or natural. The Sun shines on
the jungle, you know, on the tundra
the sea, the ghetto. Wherever you were
I knew it and saw you moving. I was waiting
for you to get to work.

               And now that you
are making your own days, so to speak,
even if no one reads you but me
you won't be depressed. Not
everyone can look up, even at me. It
hurts their eyes.'

          'Oh Sun, I'm so grateful to you!'

'Thanks and remember I'm watching. It's
easier for me to speak to you out
here. I don't have to slide down
between buildings to get your ear.
I know you love Manhattan, but
you ought to look up more often.
                                    And
always embrace things, people earth
sky stars, as I do, freely and with
the appropriate sense of space. That
is your inclination, known in the heavens
and you should follow it to hell, if
necessary, which I doubt.
                          Maybe we'll
speak again in Africa, of which I too
am specially fond. Go back to sleep now
Frank, and I may leave a tiny poem
in that brain of yours as my farewell.'

'Sun, don't go!' I was awake
at last. 'No, go I must, they're calling
me.'
        'Who are they?'
                          Rising he said 'Some
day you'll know. They're calling to you
too.' Darkly he rose, and then I slept.

FRANK O'HARA

Prayer

God give me strength to lead a double life.
Cut me in half.
Make each half happy in its own way
with what is left. Let me disobey
my own best instincts

and do what I want to do, whatever that may be,
without regretting it, or thinking I might.

When I come home late at night from home,
saying I have to go away,
remind me to look out the window
to see which house I'm in.
Pin a smile on my face
when I turn up two weeks later with a tan
and presents for everyone.

Teach me how to stand and where to look
when I say the words
about where I've been
and what sort of time I've had.
Was it good or bad or somewhere in between?
I'd like to know how I feel about these things,
perhaps you'd let me know?

When it's time to go to bed in one of my lives,
go ahead of me up the stairs,
shine a light in the corners of my room.
Tell me this: do I wear pyjamas here,
or sleep with nothing on?
If you can't oblige by cutting me in half,
God give me strength to lead a double life.

HUGO WILLIAMS

A Priest in the Sabbath Dawn Addresses His Somnolent Mistress

Wake up, my heart, get out of bed
and put your scarlet shirt back on and leave,
for Sunday is coming down the chimney
with its feet in little socks,
and I need a space in which to write my sermon.

Although the hour's already late
it can still be done, if only you'll depart!
Down the pipe and out across the lawn
would take you to the station yard
in which you left your bicycle last week
and give me time to clothe in flesh the text
I have in mind for the instruction of my flock.
Please hurry, dear. The earliest note of the matin bell
has left its tower like an urgent dove
and is beating its way to woods outside the town.
The sun is up, the parish breakfasted,
the ghosts are all returned into the flint
yet still you lie here, shaming me with sleep.
Wake up, I say, for Sabbath legs
are landing in the grate. Go naked if you must
but grant me these few minutes with my pen
to write of how I cut myself while shaving.
Be useful, at least, and fetch my very razor,
for the faithful have set their feet upon the road
and are hurrying here with claims on the kind of story
which I cannot fittingly make from your sudden grin.

PETER DIDSBURY

Stealing

The most unusual thing I ever stole? A snowman.
Midnight. He looked magnificent; a tall, white mute
beneath the winter moon. I wanted him, a mate
with a mind as cold as the slice of ice
within my own brain. I started with the head.

Better off dead than giving in, not taking
what you want. He weighed a ton; his torso,
frozen stiff, hugged to my chest, a fierce chill

piercing my gut. Part of the thrill was knowing
that children would cry in the morning. Life's tough.

Sometimes I steal things I don't need. I joy-ride cars
to nowhere, break into houses just to have a look.
I'm a mucky ghost, leave a mess, maybe pinch a camera.
I watch my gloved hand twisting the doorknob.
A stranger's bedroom. Mirrors. I sigh like this – *Aah*.

It took some time. Reassembled in the yard,
he didn't look the same. I took a run
and booted him. Again. Again. My breath ripped out
in rags. It seems daft now. Then I was standing
alone amongst lumps of snow, sick of the world.

Boredom. Mostly I'm so bored I could eat myself.
One time, I stole a guitar and thought I might
learn to play. I nicked a bust of Shakespeare once,
flogged it, but the snowman was strangest.
You don't understand a word I'm saying, do you?

CAROL ANN DUFFY

The Congress of the Insomniacs

Mother of God, everyone is invited:
Stargazing Peruvian shepherds,
Old men on sidewalks of New York.
You, too, doll with eyes open
Listening to the rain next to a sleeping child.

A big hotel ballroom with mirrors on every side.
Think about it as you lie in the dark.
Angels on its ornate ceilings,
Naked nymphs in what must be paradise.

There's a stage, a lectern,
An usher with a flashlight.

Someone will address this gathering yet
From his bed of nails.
Sleeplessness is like metaphysics.
Be there.

CHARLES SIMIC

Mama Dot Learns to Fly

Mama Dot watched reels of film
Of inventor after inventor trying to fly.
She's so old, she's a spectator in some.

Seeing them leap off bridges straight
Into rivers, or burn
Strapped to backfiring rockets,

Or flap about with huge wings
Only to raise a whole heap of dust,
Makes her cringe: what conviction!

How misguided. Right then, she wants
To see an ancestor, in Africa; half-way
Round the world and back through time.

Her equipment's straightforward,
Thought-up to bring the lot
To her: *Come, leh we gaff girl.*

FRED D'AGUIAR

Seeing Off a Friend

Early April on Broadway, south of Union Square,
a man jumps from a twentieth floor. I
stop him at the tenth. Tell me, I say,
what have you learned in your travels?

We sit and rest awhile. I have only
just asked the question, he says. The answer
will come to me later. He smiles shyly
and continues falling to the fifth floor
where I stop him again. Tell me, I say,
what have you learned in your travels?
He smiles again, being basically cheerful,
but shakes his head. These answers
are slow in approaching, he says,
perhaps it is too soon to tell.
                              Beneath us
the crowd is clamoring for his arrival.
They shout and clap their hands in unison.
They would sing songs of welcome
if they knew them. They would beat drums.
I shrug and let him continue. He falls,
twisting silently. He nicks a streetlight,
smashing it. He hits the hood of a blue
Chevrolet, smashing it. He bounces thirty feet
and hits a parking meter, smashing it.
He lies there as people run toward him.
Their hands are open like shopping bags.
Their mouths are open like pits in the earth.
All his answers cover their faces.

STEPHEN DOBYNS

What the Doctor Said

He said it doesn't look good
he said it looks bad in fact real bad
he said I counted thirty-two of them on one lung before
I quit counting them
I said I'm glad I wouldn't want to know
about any more being there than that

he said are you a religious man do you kneel down
in forest groves and let yourself ask for help
when you come to a waterfall
mist blowing against your face and arms
do you stop and ask for understanding at those moments
I said not yet but I intend to start today
he said I'm real sorry he said
I wish I had some other kind of news to give you
I said Amen and he said something else
I didn't catch and not knowing what else to do
and not wanting him to have to repeat it
and me to have to fully digest it
I just looked at him
for a minute and he looked back it was then
I jumped up and shook hands with this man who'd just given
    me
something no one else on earth had ever given me
I may even have thanked him habit being so strong

RAYMOND CARVER

The Trees

The trees inside are moving out into the forest,
the forest that was empty all these days
where no bird could sit
no insect hide
no sun bury its feet in shadow
the forest that was empty all these nights
will be full of trees by morning.

All night the roots work
to disengage themselves from the cracks
in the veranda floor.
The leaves strain toward the glass
small twigs stiff with exertion

long-cramped boughs shuffling under the roof
like newly discharged patients
half-dazed, moving
to the clinic doors.

I sit inside, doors open to the veranda
writing long letters
in which I scarcely mention the departure
of the forest from the house.
The night is fresh, the whole moon shines
in a sky still open
the smell of leaves and lichen
still reaches like a voice into the rooms.
My head is full of whispers
which tomorrow will be silent.

Listen. The glass is breaking.
The trees are stumbling forward
into the night. Winds rush to meet them.
The moon is broken like a mirror,
its pieces flash now in the crown
of the tallest oak.

ADRIENNE RICH

For and Against the Environment

I have come out to smell the hyacinths which again in this
　　North London garden

have performed a wonderful feat of chemistry and hauled that
　　delectable perfume

out of the blackish confection of clay and potsherds which
　　feebly responds when I name it flower-bed;

and so wet was the Spring that I clipped the grass with shears,
　　to prevent the mower sliding in mud,

and my attempt to dig the beds to enhance their fertility
foundered caked with clods.

But today the April sun blazes from a cloudless sky, and the
lawn, drenched with raindrops

like an utterly saturated sponge has unfurled and surrendered
its freight,

and – where do they come from? – the small pert insects
emerge onto the skin of dryness

like Noah's prospecting pigeon and at once they are up to all
sorts of business,

and the buds you had thought paralysed if not embalmed are
surely discernibly plumper

and purpler or pinker than you remember them yesterday, and
the hum of potential life

swells with its distinctive excitement to just short of the
threshold of actual audibility

through which it bursts, perhaps, by way of the throat of that
unceasing ingenious blackbird

poised on my neighbour's gutter against the blue of the sky. O,
wonderful world!

and here are two absolute flowers, new as babies:

they have bowed their heads for weeks in their bashful, fleecy
pods,

but today they stare up at me bravely, giving all they have got

and making at last no pretence they are anything else but
anemones

and this is their hour, and if they don't impress now they will
never impress,

but they do, and to support my judgment a small fly is
   clambering deliberately over the organ stops of their
   stamens

making, I do not doubt, marvellous music. O, wonderful world!

And the ant is rushing at immense speed over the lifeless plains
   of the rose-bed

which are not plains to her but ridged and crested with salts
   and terrible canyons

and she winds every which way through them but never forgets
   her sense of direction

for she is not such a fool as to think, but attends to the sun
   and the earth's magnetism

and I am shocked by my own thought, that my own thought

may be a blind lobe on the body of the great creature of
   evolution,

an experiment which does not carry the future. And meanwhile
   here is this ant,

only the most distant relation of Mozart and Shakespeare, yet
   unmistakably designed for survival,

nosing about through the clods like an exceptionally fleet piece
   of earth-moving equipment

and not in the least reciprocating the warm concern she has
   evoked in me,

and the same is true of the blackbird, whose song I salute, and
   the anemone

whose sleek pods I have fondled, and the clods which I have
   rendered more fertile,

and at this moment, speaking now as one of the Lords of
   Creation,

speaking as one of the Shepherds of Being, unique bearers of
    conscious and self-conscious life,

I have to declare my preference within all the sparkling welter

(O, wonderful world!) and I do, keeping the ant firmly fixed in
    my gaze:

great and more fragile is man than ant or earth or anemone

and in or out of the glass-house of nature, let him above all not
    be seduced.

    D. M. BLACK

Not Being Oedipus

Not being Oedipus he did not question the Sphinx
Nor allow it to question him. He thought it expedient
To make friends and try to influence it.
In this he entirely succeeded,

And continued his journey to Thebes. The abominable thing
Now tame as a kitten (though he was not unaware
That its destructive claws were merely sheathed)
Lolloped along beside him –

To the consternation of the Reception Committee.
It posed a nice problem: he had certainly overcome
But not destroyed the creature – was he or was he not
Entitled to the hand of the Princess

Dowager Jocasta? Not being Oedipus
He saw it as a problem too. For frankly he was not
By natural instinct at all attracted to her.
The question was soon solved –

Solved itself, you might say; for while they argued
The hungry Sphinx, which had not been fed all day,

Sneaked off unobserved, penetrated the royal apartments,
And softly consumed the lady.

So he ascended the important throne of Cadmus,
Beginning a distinguished and uneventful reign.
Celibate, he had nothing to fear from ambitious sons;
Although he was lonely at nights,

With only the Sphinx, curled up upon his eiderdown.
Its body exuded a sort of unearthly warmth
(Though in fact cold-blooded) but its capacity
For affection was strictly limited.

Granted, after his death it was inconsolable,
And froze into its own stone effigy
Upon his tomb. But this was self-love, really –
It felt it had failed in its mission.

While Thebes, by common consent of the people, adopted
His extremely liberal and reasonable constitution,
Which should have enshrined his name – but not being
    Oedipus,
It vanished from history, as from legend.

JOHN HEATH-STUBBS

Water

If I were called in
To construct a religion
I should make use of water.

Going to church
Would entail a fording
To dry, different clothes;

My liturgy would employ
Images of sousing,
A furious devout drench,

And I should raise in the east
A glass of water
Where any-angled light
Would congregate endlessly.

PHILIP LARKIN

Naked Vision

I was sent to fetch an eye
promised for a fresh corneal graft.
At the doctor's rooms nurse gave me
a common paper bag;
in that, a sterile jar;
in that, the disembodied eye.

I sat in Davey Street
on a low brick garden wall
and looked. The eye looked back.
It gazed, lucid and whole,
from its colourless solution.
The window of whose soul?

Trees in St David's Park
refreshed the lunchtime lovers:
riesling gold, claret dark;
late flowers flaunted all colours.
But my friend and I had eyes
only for one another.

GWEN HARWOOD

Finale

The cruellest thing they did
was to send home his teeth from the hospital.

What could she do with those,
arriving as they did days after the funeral?

Wrapped them in one of his clean handkerchiefs
she'd laundered and taken down.
All she could do was cradle them in her hands;
they looked so strange, alone –

utterly jawless in a constant smile
not in the least like his. She could cry no more.
At midnight she took heart and aim and threw
them out of the kitchen-door.

It rocketed out, that finally-parted smile,
into the gully? the scrub? the neighbour's land?
And she went back and fell into stupid sleep,
knowing him dead at last, and by her hand.

JUDITH WRIGHT

The Big Words

The first time I heard
Transubstantiation
My head fell off.

'Explain it,' the teacher said.
I looked around the classroom
Searching for my severed head
And found it near a mouse-hole
Where we used to drop
Crumbs of bread
Turning to turds
Twice as transcendental
As holy words.

'Explain it to me,' I said to my father.
From behind the great spread pages of *The Irish Independent*

'It's a miracle,' he said,
'I'm reading John D. Hickey on the semi-final
But come back later and we'll see
What's happening to Gussie Goose and Curly Wee.'

I found out what *Transubstantiation* meant.
I trotted out my answer
But the trot turned into a gallop
And I found myself witnessing a race
Between all the big words
Used by all the small men.
I use them myself, of course,
Especially when I have nothing to say,
When I cannot raise dust or hackles, go to town, or make hay
With the little bit of life in my head
Suggesting I should drink the best wine,
Eat the best bread
And thus, with a deft flick of my mind,
Transfigure the blackest hours
On this most holy ground
Where some would make their god
Hide behind big words,
Shields to stop him showing the colour of his blood
And be safe as the bland masters of jargon
Whose blindness is an appetite
For whacking great vocabularies
That cough resoundingly
In some bottomless pit
Of self-importance.

Some night soon, I'm going to have a party
For all the big words.
By the light of a semantic moon
I'll turn the race into a dance,
And with my little words
Both hosts and servants
Catering beyond their best

For even the teeniest need
Of every resonant guest,
Big and small will all be thrilled to see
Exactly what has happened
To Gussie Goose and Curly Wee.

BRENDAN KENNELLY

The Tough Guy of London

Seen from within a heated room,
On a sunny February afternoon,
London looks like
Any other summer's day.

Step out in only
Your shirt and trousers
And, even, with a black belt in *karate*,
An invisible tough guy
With blimey cold hands and feet,
Punches you
Smack on the nose
Straight back in.

KOJO GYINYE KYEI

Depressed by a Book of Bad Poetry, I Walk Toward an Unused Pasture and Invite the Insects to Join Me

Relieved, I let the book fall behind a stone.
I climb a slight rise of grass.
I do not want to disturb the ants
Who are walking single file up the fence post,
Carrying small white petals,
Casting shadows so frail that I can see through them.

I close my eyes for a moment, and listen.
The old grasshoppers
Are tired, they leap heavily now,
Their thighs are burdened.
I want to hear them, they have clear sounds to make.
Then lovely, far off, a dark cricket begins
In the maple trees.

JAMES WRIGHT

The Beast in the Space

Shut up. Shut up. There's nobody here.
If you think you hear somebody knocking
On the other side of the words, pay
No attention. It will be only
The great creature that thumps its tail
On silence on the other side.
If you do not even hear that
I'll give the beast a quick skelp
And through Art you'll hear it yelp.

The beast that lives on silence takes
Its bite out of either side.
It pads and sniffs between us. Now
It comes and laps my meaning up.
Call it over. Call it across
This curious necessary space.
Get off, you terrible inhabiter
Of silence. I'll not have it. Get
Away to whoever it is will have you.

He's gone and if he's gone to you
That's fair enough. For on this side
Of the words it's late. The heavy moth
Bangs on the pane. The whole house

Is sleeping and I remember
I am not here, only the space
I sent the terrible beast across.
Watch. He bites. Listen gently
To any song he snorts or growls
And give him food. He means neither
Well or ill towards you. Above
All, shut up. Give him your love.

W. S. GRAHAM

What the Chairman Told Tom

Poetry? It's a hobby.
I run model trains.
Mr Shaw there breeds pigeons.

It's not work. You dont sweat.
Nobody pays for it.
You *could* advertise soap.

Art, that's opera; or repertory—
The Desert Song.
Nancy was in the chorus.

But to ask for twelve pounds a week—
married, aren't you?—
you've got a nerve.

How could I look a bus conductor
in the face
if I paid you twelve pounds?

Who says it's poetry, anyhow?
My ten year old
can do it *and* rhyme.

I get three thousand and expenses,
a car, vouchers,
but I'm an accountant.

They do what I tell them,
my company.
What do *you* do?

Nasty little words, nasty long words,
it's unhealthy.
I want to wash when I meet a poet.

They're Reds, addicts,
all delinquents.
What you write is rot.

Mr Hines says so, and he's a schoolteacher,
he ought to know.
Go and find *work*.

BASIL BUNTING

Acknowledgements

This book could not have been put together without the assistance of Mary Enright and her staff at the South Bank Centre's Poetry Library, and the wealth of poetry on the shelves there.

J.S., M.S.

The editors and publishers gratefully acknowledge permissions to use copyright material in this book as follows:

FLEUR ADCOCK: to Oxford University Press for 'A Surprise in the Peninsula' and 'Against Coupling' from *Selected Poems* (1983). JOHN AGARD: to Serpent's Tail Press for 'Palm Tree King' from *Mangoes and Bullets*, copyright © John Agard, 1987. MONIZA ALVI: to Oxford University Press for 'Houdini' from *A Bowl of Warm Air* (1996); originally published in *Poetry Review*, Vol. 84, No. 1, Spring 1994. SIMON ARMITAGE: to Faber and Faber Ltd for 'Hitcher' from *Book of Matches* (1993), and 'Before You Cut Loose' from *The Dead Sea Poems* (1995). JOHN ASH: to Carcanet Press Ltd for 'The Monuments' from *Disbelief* (1987). JOHN ASHBERY: to Carcanet Press Ltd for 'The Painter' from *Selected Poems* (1986). W. H. AUDEN: to Faber and Faber Ltd for 'Moon Landing' from *Selected Poems* (1979). GEORGE AWOONOR-WILLIAMS: to Peter Owen Ltd for 'The Sea Eats the Land at Home' from *African/English Literature*. EDWARD BAUGH: to the author for 'Nigger Sweat' from *Crossing Waters: Contemporary Poetry of the English-Speaking Caribbean* (Greenfield Review, 1992). PATRICIA BEER: to Carcanet Press Ltd for 'A Dream of Hanging' from *Selected Poems* (Hutchinson, 1979). JOHN BERRYMAN: to Faber and Faber Ltd for 'Henry by Night' from *Collected Poems 1937–1971* and 'Dream Songs' (4, 63) from *The Dream Songs*. SUJATA BHATT: to Carcanet Press Ltd for 'Looking Up'. ELIZABETH BISHOP: to Farrar Straus & Giroux Inc for 'Bight' and 'Crusoe in England' from *The Complete Poems 1927–1979*, copyright © 1979, 1983 by Alice Helen Methfessel. D. M. BLACK: to Polygon Publishers for 'The Red Judge' and 'For and Against the Environment' from *Selected Poems 1964–1987* (1991). EAVAN BOLAND: to Carcanet Press Ltd for 'The Emigrant Irish' from *Collected Poems*. CHARLES BOYLE: to Faber and Faber Ltd for 'Species' from *Paleface* (1996). EDWARD KAMAU BRATHWAITE: to Oxford University Press Ltd for 'The Making of the Drum' from *The Arrivants* (1973). GEORGE MACKAY BROWN: to John Murray (Publishers) Ltd for 'Hamnavoe Market' from *Selected Poems*. BASIL BUNTING: to Oxford University Press Ltd for 'What the Chairman Told Tom' from *The Complete Poems of Basil Bunting* (1994).

Berlin Wall Café, first published in 1985 by The Blackstaff Press Ltd, new edition published in 1995 by The Harvill Press, copyright © Paul Durcan 1985, 1988, 1993, 1995. D. J. ENRIGHT: to Oxford University Press Ltd and Watson, Little Ltd as the licensing agents for 'Dreaming in the Shanghai Restaurant' from *Collected Poems* (1981). GAVIN EWART: to Mrs M. A. Ewart for 'Warm to the Cuddly-toy Charm of a Koala Bear' and 'Dream of a Slave' from *The Collected Ewart 1933–1980* (Hutchinson). NISSIM EZEKIEL: to Oxford University Press (India) for 'The Patriot' from *Collected Poems 1952–1988*. U. A. FANTHORPE: to the author for 'Not My Best Side' and 'Portraits of Tudor Statesmen' from *Side Effects* and *Standing To* (Peterloo Poets). VICKI FEAVER: to Random House UK Ltd for 'Lily Pond' from *The Handless Maiden* (Cape, 1984). JAMES FENTON: to the Peters, Fraser & Dunlop Group Ltd for 'The Ballad of the Shrieking Man' from *Out of Danger* (Penguin, 1993). ROY FISHER: to Oxford University Press Ltd for 'A Sign Illuminated' from *Birmingham River* (1994). ROBERT FROST: to Random House UK Ltd on behalf of the Estate of Robert Frost for 'Draft Horse' from *The Poetry of Robert Frost*, ed. Edward Connery Lathem (Cape). ALICE FULTON: to the author and University of Illinois Press for 'My Second Marriage to My First Husband' from *Palladium*, copyright © 1986 by Alice Fulton. TESS GALLAGHER: to the author c/o Rogers, Coleridge & White Ltd., 20 Powis Mews, London W11 1JN in association with International Creative Management, 40 West 57th Street, New York, NY 10019, USA, for 'Black Silk' from *My Black Horse* (Bloodaxe), copyright © 1984 Tess Gallagher. W. S. GRAHAM: to Margaret Snow on behalf of Nessie Graham for 'The Beast in the Space' and 'Johann Joachim Quantz's Five Lessons' from *Selected Poems* (Faber), copyright © the Estate of W. S. Graham. JAMIE GRANT: to the author c/o Margaret Connolly & Associates Pty Ltd for 'Skywriting' from *Skywriting* (Angus & Robertson). ROBERT GRAVES: to Carcanet Press Ltd for 'Apple Island' and 'All Except Hannibal' from *Selected Poems* (Penguin). LAVINIA GREENLAW: to Faber and Faber Ltd for 'Love from a Foreign City' from *Night Photograph*. GEOFFREY GRIGSON: to David Higham Associates for 'Death of a Farmyard' from *Collected Poems 1963–1980* (Allison & Busby). MARILYN HACKER: to the author for 'Oh little one, this longing is the pits' from *Love, Death and the Changing of the Seasons* (Onlywomen Press), copyright ©Marilyn Hacker, 1986. TONY HARRISON: to the author for 'Timer' and 'The Bright Lights of Sarajevo'. MICHAEL HARTNETT: to The Gallery Press for 'Death of an Irishwoman' from *Selected and New Poems* (1994). GWEN HARWOOD: to Oxford University Press for 'Cups' and 'Hospital Evening' from

Collected Poems (1991); to HarperCollins Publishers Australia for 'Naked Vision' from *The Lion's Bride* (Angus & Robertson). SEAMUS HEANEY: to Faber and Faber Ltd for 'A Sofa in the Forties' from *The Spirit Level*, 'A Constable Calls' and 'Punishment' from *North*, and 'Lightenings' (viii) from *Seeing Things*. JOHN HEATH-STUBBS: to David Higham Associates for 'Not Being Oedipus' from *Collected Poems* (Carcanet). ANTHONY HECHT: to Oxford University Press Ltd and Alfred A. Knopf Inc. for 'More Light! More Light!' and 'Behold the Lilies of the Field' from *Collected Earlier Poems* (1991), copyright © 1990 by Anthony Hecht. MICHAEL HEFFERNAN: to University of Arkansas Press for 'Presidents' from *The Man at Home*, copyright © Michael Heffernan 1988. SELIMA HILL: to Bloodaxe Books for 'Being a Wife' from *Trembling Hearts in the Bodies of Dogs* (Bloodaxe, 1994). MICHAEL HOFMANN: to Faber and Faber Ltd for 'Ancient Evenings' from *Acrimony* (1986). CHRISTOPHER HOPE: to the author c/o Rogers, Coleridge & White Ltd for 'In the Country of the Black Pig' from *The Black Pig* (London Magazine Editions), copyright © 1995 by Christopher Hope. TED HUGHES: to Faber and Faber Ltd for 'The Other', 'You Hated Spain' and 'An October Salmon' from *New Selected Poems 1957–1994*, and 'A Grin' from *Crow*. KATHLEEN JAMIE: to Bloodaxe Books for 'Mr and Mrs Scotland Are Dead' from *The Queen of Sheba* (1994). DONALD JUSTICE: to Alfred A. Knopf Inc for 'Variations for Two Pianos' from *New and Selected Poems*, copyright © 1995 by Donald Justice. PATRICK KAVANAGH: to the Trustees of the Estate of Patrick Kavanagh c/o Peter Fallon, Literary Agent, Loughcrew, Oldcastle, Co. Meath, Ireland, for 'The Hospital' from *Come Dance with Kitty Strobling*. JACKIE KAY: to Bloodaxe Books for 'Dance of the Cherry Blossom' from *The Adoption Papers* (1991). BRENDAN KENNELLY: to Bloodaxe Books Ltd for 'The Big Words' from *Time for Voices* (Bloodaxe, 1990). GALWAY KINNELL: to Alfred A. Knopf Inc for 'Oatmeal' from *When One Has Lived a Long Time Alone*, copyright © 1990 by Galway Kinnell. AUGUST KLEINZAHLER: to the author for 'Green Sees Things in Waves' (*London Review of Books*). ARUN KOLATKAR: to Clearing House, Bombay, for 'A Low Temple' and 'The Railway Station' from *Jejuri* (1976). PHILIP LARKIN: to Faber and Faber Ltd for 'The Old Fools', 'Water' and 'The Explosion' from *Collected Poems*. GEOFFREY LEHMANN: to Curtis Brown Australia Pty Ltd for 'Harold's Walk' from *Children's Games* (Angus & Robertson, 1990). PHILIP LEVINE: to Alfred A. Knopf Inc. for 'What Work Is' from *What Work Is*, copyright © 1991 by Philip Levine, and 'Listen Carefully' from *The Simple Truth*, copyright © 1994 by Philip Levine. LIZ LOCHHEAD: to

Polygon Publishers for 'My Rival's House' from *Dreaming Frankenstein*. CHRISTOPHER LOGUE: to Faber and Faber Ltd for 'Rat, O Rat' from *Selected Poems*. MICHAEL LONGLEY: to Reed Consumer Books for 'Ghetto' from *Gorse Fires* (Secker & Warburg); to Random House UK Ltd for 'The Scissors Ceremony' from *The Ghost Orchid* (Cape). ROBERT LOWELL: to Faber and Faber Ltd for 'Memories of West Street and Lepke' and 'Skunk Hour' from *Life Studies*. THOMAS LYNCH: to Random House UK Ltd for 'Maura' and 'Grimalkin' from *Grimalkin* (Cape). GEORGE MACBETH: to Sheil Land Associates Ltd for 'Owl', 'Bedtime Story' and 'The God of Love' from *Collected Poems 1958–1982* (Hutchinson, 1989). NORMAN MACCAIG: to Random House UK Ltd on behalf of the estate of the author for 'Notations of Ten Summer Minutes' and 'Sleeping Compartment' from *Collected Poems* (Chatto, 1985). ROGER MCGOUGH: to the Peters, Fraser & Dunlop Group Ltd for 'Defying Gravity' from *Defying Gravity* (Penguin). HEATHER MCHUGH: to University Press of New England for 'Coming' from *Hinge & Sign* (Wesleyan University Press), copyright © 1994 by Heather McHugh. LOUIS MACNEICE: to David Higham Associates Ltd for 'The Taxis' and 'Soap Suds' from *Collected Poems* (Faber). SARAH MAGUIRE: to Reed Consumer Books for 'Spilt Milk' from *Spilt Milk* (Secker & Warburg). DEREK MAHON: to Oxford University Press for 'A Disused Shed in County Wexford', 'As It Should Be' and 'Lives' from *Poems 1962–1978* (1979). BILL MANHIRE: to Carcanet Press for 'Out West' from *Milky Way Bar* (1991). E. A. MARKHAM: to the author for 'The Sea' from *Human Rites: Selected Poems 1970–1982* (Anvil Press Poetry, 1982). WILLIAM MATTHEWS: to Houghton Mifflin Company for 'Onions' from *Blues If You Want*, copyright © 1989 by William Matthews. PAULA MEEHAN: to The Gallery Press for 'Child Burial' from *The Man Who Was Marked by Winter* (1991). ADRIAN MITCHELL: to the Peters, Fraser and Dunlop Group Ltd for 'Fifteen Million Plastic Bags' from *For Beauty Douglas* (Allison & Busby Ltd, 1982); none of Adrian Mitchell's poems are to be used in any examination whatsoever. SUSAN MITCHELL: to Harper Collins Publishers Inc. for 'Smoke' from *Rapture*, copyright © 1992 by Susan Mitchell. EDWIN MORGAN: to Carcanet Press for 'From the Domain of Arnheim' and 'The Video Box: 25' from *Collected Poems*. EDWIN MUIR: to Faber and Faber Ltd for 'The Horses' from *Collected Poems*. PAUL MULDOON: to Faber and Faber Ltd for 'The Birth' from *The Annals of Chile*, 'Why Brownlee Left' from *Why Brownlee Left*, and 'Meeting the British' from *Meeting the British*. LES MURRAY: to Carcanet Press for 'The Broad Bean Sermon' and 'The Quality of Sprawl' from *Collected Poems*, 'The Dream of Wearing Shorts Forever' from *The Daylight Moon*, and 'The Transposition of Clermont' from *Dog Fox Field*. NORMAN NICHOLSON: to David Higham Associates for 'The Tune the Old Cow Died of' from *Collected Poems* (Faber). SEAN O'BRIEN: to Oxford University Press Ltd for 'Before' from *HMS Glasshouse* (1991). FRANK O'HARA: to Carcanet Press for 'A True Account...' from *Selected Poems*. SHARON OLDS: to Reed Consumer Books for 'Ecstasy' and 'I Go Back to May 1937' from *The Sign of Saturn* (Secker & Warburg). MICHAEL ONDAATJE: to Marion Boyars Publishers Ltd for 'Rat Jelly' and 'The Strange Case' from *Rat Jelly and Other Poems 1963–1978*. RUTH PADEL: to Bloodaxe Books for 'On the Venom Farm' from *Angel* (1993). DON PATERSON: to Faber and Faber Ltd for 'A Private Bottling' from *God's Gift to Women*. TOM PAULIN: to Faber and Faber Ltd for 'The Sting' from *Walking a Line*. KATHERINE PIERPOINT: to Faber and Faber Ltd for 'This Dead Relationship' from *Truffle Beds*. ROBERT PINSKY: to The Ecco Press for 'From the Childhood of Jesus' from *The Want Bone*, © 1990 by Robert Pinsky. SYLVIA PLATH: to Faber and Faber Ltd for 'Applicant', 'Death & Co', 'Balloons' and 'Cut' from *Ariel*. PETER PORTER: to Oxford University Press Ltd for 'The King of the Cats is Dead' and 'A Consumer's Report' from *Collected Poems* (1983). CRAIG RAINE: to Faber and Faber Ltd for 'The Man Who Invented Pain' from *Rich* (1983). A. K. RAMANUJAN: to Oxford University Press Ltd for 'Routine Day Sonnet' from *Relations*. PETER READING: to Bloodaxe Books for 'Ye haue heard this yarn afore' from *Collected Poems 2: 1985–1996* (1996). PETER REDGROVE: to David Higham Associates Ltd for 'Song' and 'The Visible Baby' from *The Moon Disposes: Poems 1954–1987* (Secker & Warburg, 1987). ADRIENNE RICH: to the author and W. W. Norton & Company, Inc., for 'Diving into the Wreck' (copyright © 1975, 1978 by W. W. Norton & Company, Inc., copyright © 1981 by Adrienne Rich) from *The Fact of a Doorframe: Poems Selected and New, 1950–1984*, copyright © 1984 by Adrienne Rich, and for 'The Trees', 'Two Songs' and 'Not Like That' (all copyright © 1993 by Adrienne Rich, copyright © 1966 by W. W. Norton & Company, Inc.) from *Collected Early Poems: 1950–1970*. MAURICE RIORDAN: to Faber and Faber Ltd for 'Time Out' from *A Word from the Loki*. THEODORE ROETHKE: to Faber and Faber Ltd for 'The Geranium' from *The Collected Poems of Theodore Roethke*. NEIL ROLLINSON: to Random House UK Ltd for 'The Ecstasy of St Saviour's Avenue' from *A Spillage of Mercury* (Cape). CAROL RUMENS: to Bloodaxe Books for 'From a Conversation During Divorce' from *Best China Sky* (1995). OLIVER SENIOR: to Bloodaxe Books for 'Brief Lives' from *Gardening in the Tropics* (1986). ANNE SEXTON: to the Peters, Fraser & Dunlop Group

Ltd for 'Red Roses' from *The Complete Poems* (Houghton Mifflin), copyright © 1976 by Anne Sexton. CHARLES SIMIC: to Faber and Faber Ltd for 'Popular Mechanics', 'The Congress of the Insomniacs' and 'Country Fair' from *Frightening Toys*, to Reed Consumer Books for 'Austerities' from *Austerities* (Secker & Warburg) and to George Braziller Inc. for 'My Shoes' from *Selected Poems* (1985). LOUIS SIMPSON: to the author for 'Outward' from *Selected Poems* and 'The Silent Piano' from *Adventures of the Letter I*. DAVE SMITH: to the author for 'An American Roadside Elegy' from *Cuba Night* (William Morrow, 1990), copyright Dave Smith. STEVIE SMITH: to James MacGibbon for 'Not Waving but Drowning' and 'Black March' from *The Collected Poems of Stevie Smith* (Penguin). BERNARD SPENCER: to Oxford University Press Ltd for 'Boat Poem' from *Collected Poems* (1981). ELIZABETH SPIRES: to the author for 'The Woman on the Dump' from *Annonciade* (Viking Penguin Inc.). WALLACE STEVENS: to Faber and Faber Ltd for 'The Plain Sense of Things' from *The Collected Poems of Wallace Stevens*. MARK STRAND: to Alfred A. Knopf Inc for 'Always' from *The Continuous Life*, copyright © 1990 by Mark Strand; to Carcanet Press for 'Where Are the Waters of Childhood?' from *Selected Poems*. JAMES TATE: to University Press of New England for 'The Lost Pilot' from *Selected Poems* (Wesleyan University Press), copyright © 1991 by James Tate, and to the author for 'I Am a Finn' and 'I Am Still a Finn' from *Distance from Loved Ones* (Wesleyan University Press, 1990). R. S. THOMAS: to Orion Publishing Group Ltd for 'The Empty Church' from *Collected Poems 1945–1990* (J.M. Dent); to Carcanet Press for 'Raptor' from *No Truce with the Furies* (1995). CHASE TWICHELL: to Faber and Faber Ltd for 'Aisle of Dogs' from *The Ghost of Eden*, and 'The Condom Tree' from *Perdido*. DEREK WALCOTT: to Faber and Faber Ltd for 'The Season of Phantasmal Peace' from *Collected Poems 1948–1984*. BELLE WARING: to University of Pittsburgh Press for 'When a Beautiful Woman Gets on the Jutiapa Bus' from *Refuge*, copyright © 1990 by Belle Waring. SUSAN WICKS: to Faber and Faber Ltd for 'The Knot' from *The Clever Daughter*. RICHARD WILBUR: to Faber and Faber Ltd for 'Shame' from *New and Collected Poems*. C. K. WILLIAMS: to Sheil Land Associates Ltd for 'My Mother's Lips' from *Poems 1963–1983* (Bloodaxe). HUGO WILLIAMS: to Faber and Faber Ltd for 'Prayer' from *Dock Leaves*; to Oxford University Press Ltd for 'When I Grow Up' from *Self-Portrait with a Slide* (1990). JOHN HARTLEY WILLIAMS: to Bloodaxe Books Ltd for 'Script Conference' from *Bright River Yonder* (Bloodaxe, 1987). WILLIAM CARLOS WILLIAMS: to Carcanet Press for 'The Turtle' from *Collected Poems*. GERARD WOODWARD: to Random House UK for

'Lighthouse' from *After the Deafening* (Chatto & Windus, 1994).
JAMES WRIGHT: to University Press of New England for 'Two Hangovers' and 'Depressed by a Book of Bad Poetry' from *Above the River* (Wesleyan University Press), copyright © 1990 by James Wright.
JUDITH WRIGHT: to Carcanet Press for 'Finale' from *Collected Poems*.
KIT WRIGHT: to Random House UK Ltd for 'A Doll's House' from *Poems '74–'83* (Hutchinson).

Every effort has been made to contact all copyright holders. The publishers would be grateful to be notified of any additions that should be incorporated in the next edition of this volume.

Index of Poets

Adcock, Fleur (b. Auckland, New Zealand, 1934), 67, 150

Agard, John (b. Guyana, 1949), 29

Alvi, Moniza (b. Lahore, Pakistan, 1954), 234

Armitage, Simon (b. Huddersfield, Yorkshire, 1963), 144, 157

Ash, John (b. Manchester, 1948), 125

Ashbery, John (b. Rochester, New York, 1927), 89

Auden, W. H. (b. York, 1907–73), 86

Awoonor-Williams, George (b. Ghana, 1935), 108

Baugh, Edward (b. Jamaica, 1936), 163

Beer, Patricia (b. Exmouth, Devon, 1924), 137

Berry, James (b. Boston, Jamaica, 1924), 129

Berryman, John (b. McAlester, Oklahoma, 1914–72), 116, 117

Bhatt, Sujata (b. Ahmedabad, India, 1956), 238

Bishop, Elizabeth (b. Worcester, Massachusetts, 1911–79), 81, 120

Black, D. M. (b. Cape Town, South Africa, 1941), 96, 282

Boland, Eavan (b. Dublin, 1944), 164

Boyle, Charles (b. Leeds, 1951), 145

Brathwaite, Edward Kamau (b. Bridgetown, Barbados, 1930), 34

Brown, George Mackay (b. Orkney, 1921–96), 3

Bunting, Basil (b. Northumberland, 1900–1985), 292

Burnside, John (b. Dunfirmline, Fife, 1955), 66

Carson, Ciaran (b. Belfast, 1948), 183

Carver, Raymond (b. Clatskanie, Oregon, 1939–88), 94, 280

Causley, Charles (b. Launceston, Cornwall, 1917), 243

Chuilleanáin, Eiléan Ní (b. Co. Cork, 1942), 50, 51, 218, 252

Collins, Billy, 244

Cummings, E. E. (b. Cambridge, Massachusetts, 1894–1962), 169

Curnow, Allen (b. Timaru, New Zealand, 1911), 215

D'Aguiar, Fred (b. London, 1960), 279

Dawe, Bruce (b. Geelong, Victoria, Australia, 1930), 259

Dharker, Imtiaz (b. Lahore, Pakistan, 1954), 190

Dickey, James (b. Atlanta, Georgia, 1923), 12, 152

Didsbury, Peter (b. Fleetwood, Lancs, 1946), 11, 276

Dobyns, Stephen (b. Orange, New Jersey, 1941), 159, 279

Donaghy, Michael (b. New York, 1954), 216

Doty, Mark (b. Tennessee, 1953), 5

Dove, Rita (b. Akron, Ohio, 1952), 106

Downie, Freda (b. London, 1929–93), 169

Duffy, Carol Ann (b. Glasgow, 1955), 192, 235, 240, 277

Duhig, Ian (b. London, 1954), 265

Dunn, Douglas (b. Renfrewshire, 1942), 22

Durcan, Paul (b. Dublin, 1944), 196, 264

Enright, D. J. (b. Leamington, Warwickshire, 1920), 146

Ewart, Gavin (b. London, 1916–95), 141, 142

Ezekiel, Nissim (b. Bombay, India, 1924), 251

Fanthorpe, U. A. (b. London, 1929), 262

Feaver, Vicki (b. Nottingham, 1943), 233

Fenton, James (b. Lincoln, 1949), 130

Ferlinghetti, Lawrence (b. Yonkers, New York, 1919), 269

Fisher, Roy (b. Handsworth, Birmingham, 1930), 175

Frost, Robert (b. San Francisco, 1874–1963), 217

Fulton, Alice (b. Troy, New York, 1952), 232

Gallagher, Tess (b. Port Angeles, Washington, 1932), 272

Ginsberg, Allen (b. Newark, New Jersey, 1926), 267

Graham, W. S. (b. Greenock, 1918–86), 42, 291

Graves, Robert (b. Wimbledon, 1895–1985), 28

Grant, Jamie (b. Melbourne, Australia, 1949), 92

Greenlaw, Lavinia (b. London, 1962), 236

Grigson, Geoffrey (b. Pelynt, Cornwall, 1905–85), 176

Hacker, Marilyn (b. New York City, 1942), 73

Harrison, Tony (b. Leeds, 1937), 58, 177

Hartnett, Michael (b. Newcastle West, Co. Limerick, 1941), 245

Harwood, Gwen (b. Brisbane, Australia, 1920), 246, 287

Heaney, Seamus (b. Mossbawn, Co. Derry, 1939), 4, 54, 59, 229

Heath-Stubbs, John (b. London, 1918), 285

Hecht, Anthony (b. New York City, 1923), 21, 77

Heffernan, Michael (b. 1942), 261

Hill, Geoffrey (b. Bromsgrove, Worcestershire, 1932), 33

Hill, Selima (b. London, 1945), 149

Hofmann, Michael (b. Freiburg, Germany, 1957), 231

Hope, Christopher (b. Johannesburg, South Africa, 1944), 109

Hughes, Ted (b. Mytholmroyd, Yorkshire, 1930), 134, 218, 224, 225

Jamie, Kathleen (b. Renfrewshire, 1962), 26

Justice, Donald (b. Miami, Florida, 1925), 45

Kavanagh, Patrick (b. Inniskeen, Co. Monaghan, 1904–67), 247

Kay, Jackie (b. Edinburgh, 1961), 139

Kennelly, Brendan (b. Ballylongford, Co. Kerry, 1936), 288

Kinnell, Galway (b. Providence, Rhode Island, 1927), 199

Kleinzahler, August (b. Jersey City, 1949), 241

Kolatkar, Arun (b. Kolhapur, 1932), 126, 170

Kyei, Kojo Gyinye (b. Ghana, 1932), 290

Larkin, Philip (b. Coventry, 1922–85), 176, 222, 286

Lehmann, Geoffrey (b. Sydney, Australia, 1940), 7

Levine, Philip (b. Detroit, Michigan, 1928), 20, 249

Lochhead, Liz (b. Lanarkshire, 1947), 14

Logue, Christopher (b. Portsmouth, 1926), 13

Longley, Michael (b. Belfast, 1939), 62, 178

Lowell, Robert (b. Boston, Massachusetts, 1917–77), 118, 220

Lynch, Thomas (b. Detroit, Michigan, 1948), 76, 155

Macbeth, George (b. Shotts, Lanarkshire, 1932–92), 10, 38, 127

MacCaig, Norman (b. Edinburgh, 1910–96), 173, 228

McGough, Roger (b. Liverpool, 1937), 138

McHugh, Heather (b. California, 1948), 74

MacNeice, Louis (b. Belfast, 1907–63), 174, 228

Maguire, Sarah (b. London, 1957), 75

Mahon, Derek (b. Belfast, 1941), 56, 94, 204

Manhire, Bill (b. Invercargill, New Zealand, 1946), 204

Markham, E. A. (b. Montserrat, 1939), 254

Matthews, William (b. Cincinnati, Ohio, 1942), 198

Meehan, Paula (b. Dublin, 1955), 69

Mitchell, Adrian (b. London, 1932), 260

Mitchell, Susan (b. New York City, 1944), 18

Moraes, Dom (b. Bombay, India, 1938), 161

Morgan, Edwin (b. Glasgow, 1920), 61, 97

Motion, Andrew (b. London, 1952), 237

Muldoon, Paul (b. Portadown, Co. Armagh, 1951), 109, 217, 254

Muir, Edwin (b. Deerness, Orkney, 1887–1959), 40

Murray, Les (b. Nabiac, NSW, Australia, 1938), 32, 47, 123, 257

Nicholson, Norman (b. Millom, Cumberland, 1910–87), 248

O'Brien, Sean (b. London, 1952), 64

O'Hara, Frank (b. Baltimore, Maryland, 1926–66), 273

Ojaide, Tanure (b. Nigeria, 1948), 31, 104

Ofeimun, Odia (b. Nigeria, 1947), 87

Olds, Sharon (b. San Francisco,1942), 73, 223

Ondaatje, Michael (b. Colombo, Sri Lanka, 1943), 158, 203

Padel, Ruth (b. London, 1947), 208

Paterson, Don (b. Dundee, 1963), 187

Paulin, Tom (b. Leeds, 1949), 210

Pierpoint, Katherine (b. Northampton, 1961), 193

Pinsky, Robert (b. New Jersey, 1940), 213

Plath, Sylvia (b. Boston, Massachusetts, 1932–63), 70, 111, 140, 255

Porter, Peter (b. Brisbane, Australia, 1929), 147, 256

Raine, Craig (b. Shildon, Durham, 1944), 166

Ramanujan, A. K. (b. Mysore, India, 1929–93), 195

Reading, Peter (b. Liverpool, 1946), 79

Redgrove, Peter (b. Kingston, Surrey, 1932), 68, 143

Rich, Adrienne (b. Baltimore, Maryland, 1929), 51, 71, 135, 281

Riordan, Maurice (b. Co. Cork, 1953), 23

Roethke, Theodore (b. Saginaw, Michigan, 1908–63), 154

Rollinson, Neil (b. Keighley, Yorkshire, 1960), 151

Rumens, Carol (b. London, 1944), 197

Senior, Olive (b. Jamaica, 1943), 27

Sexton, Anne (b. Newton, Massachusetts, 1928–74), 6

Simic, Charles (b. Serbia, 1938), 100, 115, 159, 162, 278

Simpson, Louis (b. Jamaica, 1923), 38, 88

Smith, Dave (b. Portsmouth, Virginia, 1942), 46

Smith, Stevie (b. Hull, 1902–71), 113, 219

Spencer, Bernard (b. Madras, India, 1909–63), 121

Spires, Elizabeth (b. Lancaster, Ohio, 1952), 165

Stevens, Wallace (b. Reading, Pennsylvania, 1879–1955), 179

Strand, Mark (b. Prince Edward Island, Canada, 1934), 101, 179

Tate, James (b. Kansas City, Missouri, 1943), 90, 102, 103

Thomas, R. S. (b. Cardiff, 1913), 127, 212

Tonks, Rosemary (b. London, 1932), 114, 115

Twichell, Chase (b. New Haven, Connecticut, 1950), 17, 207

Walcott, Derek (b. Castries, St Lucia, 1930), 60

Waring, Belle (b. Warrenton, Virginia, 1951), 148

Wicks, Susan (b. Edenbridge, Kent, 1947), 239

Wilbur, Richard (b. New York, 1921), 110

Williams, C. K. (b. Newark, New Jersey, 1936), 181

Williams, Hugo (b. Windsor,
    Berkshire, 1942), 202, 275
Williams, John Hartley (b. Cheshire,
    1942), 205
Williams, William Carlos (b.
    Rutherford, New Jersey, 1883–
    1963), 105

Woodward, Gerard (b. London,
    1961), 99
Wright, James (b. St Martin's Ferry,
    Ohio, 1927–80), 242, 290
Wright, Judith (b. Armidale, NSW,
    Australia, 1915), 287
Wright, Kit (b. Kent, 1944), 16